Symposium on the Magisterium: A Positive Statement

Symposium on the Magisterium:

A POSITIVE STATEMENT

Co-sponsored by the
Institute of Catholic Higher Education
and the Archdiocese of Philadelphia

Commentary by S. Thomas Greenburg

Edited by Msgr. John J. O'Rourke
and S. Thomas Greenburg

ST. PAUL EDITIONS

Imprimatur:
+John Cardinal Krol
Archbishop of Philadelphia

Library of Congress Cataloging in Publication Data

Symposium on the Magisterium, Philadelphia, 1978.
   Symposium on the Magisterium.

   Symposium co-sponsored by the Archdiocese of
Philadelphia and the Institute for Catholic
Higher Education.
      1.   Catholic Church--Teaching office--Congresses.
I.   O'Rourke, John J.   II.   Philadelphia
(Archdiocese)   III.   Institute for Catholic Higher
Education.
BX1746.S87   1978   207'.11'2   78-19188

Printed in U.S.A. by the Daughters of St. Paul
50 St. Paul's Ave., Boston, Ma. 02130

The Daughters of St. Paul are an international religious congregation
serving the Church with the communications media.

CONTENTS

PREFACE

The Conciliar Decrees on Ecumenism (n.1), on Missionary Activity (n. 6) and the Apostolic Exhortation On Evangelization (n. 77) clearly state that divisions among Christians contradict the will of Christ, scandalize the world, damage the work of preaching the Gospel to every creature and deprive many people of access to the faith.

In his opening speech to the Second Vatican Council, Pope John declared that he convoked the Council for the purpose of reaffirming again the teaching authority of the Church. A month after the conclusion of the Council, Pope Paul said: "The Council is a great act of the Magisterium of the Church, and anyone who adheres to the Council is, by that very fact, recognizing and honoring the Magisterium of the Church" (January 12, 1966).

During and since the Second Vatican Council, Pope Paul found it necessary to deplore the attacks on the Church and its teaching authority. On July 7, 1965 he said: "A spirit of criticism and even indocility and rebellion is calling into question sacrosanct norms for Christian life." On December 23, 1965 he said: "The Council has not inaugurated a period of dogmatic and moral uncertainty, or of disciplinary indifference, or superficial irenicism or of organizational weakening." On February 22, 1967, in his Apostolic Exhortation *Petrum Et Paulum*, he wrote: "Catholic belief is being contaminated. Ideas are appearing in the fields of exegesis and theology which have their origin in certain bold but misleading philosophical theories which cast doubt

11

upon or narrow down the full meaning of the truths which the Church has taught with her rightful authority."

On June 20, 1977, the Pope told a group of French bishops: "It is to misunderstand seriously the meaning of the conciliar event to take it as authority for setting up a so-called theological method that would permit, in the name of creativity and freedom of research, the interpretation to each person's taste of the scriptural text, the content of tradition, and setting one's self up as a judge of the teaching and directives of the supreme authority of the Church. ...*Respect for the Magisterium is a constitutive element of theological method.* And also respect for the People of God, who have a right not to be inconsiderably troubled by adventurous hypotheses or positions, which it does not have the competence to judge or which run the risk of being simplified or manipulated by movements of opinion."

Precisely because of respect for the People of God and their right not to be troubled and scandalized, I responded favorably to the suggestion of the president of the Institute for Catholic Higher Education, Doctor S. Thomas Greenburg, that an international symposium on the Magisterium be held in Philadelphia. The Symposium, co-sponsored by the Archdiocese of Philadelphia and the Institute for Catholic Higher Education, was held in Philadelphia on January 6-8, 1978.

To insure the highest level of discussions, invitations were limited to scholars and educators. There was a general impression that the papers presented were very positive in thrust, of high order, and the discussions were stimulating. During and after the Symposium, we were urged to give a wider currency to the papers presented. The Daughters of St. Paul volunteered to print and publish the talks, which are contained in this book.

My best recommendation of this publication cannot possibly match the merits of its contents. We sincerely trust that the Symposium will help to minimize the divisions which scandalize the world and ignore the rights of the People of God to the clear, authentic teachings of faith.

John Cardinal Krol
Archbishop of Philadelphia

Feast of the Chair of St. Peter
February 22, 1978
Philadelphia

COMMENTARY

S. Thomas Greenburg
President, The Institute of Catholic Higher Education

This symposium was designed to make a positive statement on the Magisterium.

It is not our purpose to summarize what has been said by those speakers who have achieved this positive statement.

However, as one who has been deeply involved in the international debate on the problems of Catholic higher education, all of which are essentially related to the Magisterium, the writer feels obliged to suggest a *fundamental framework within which the spark that has ignited the whole debate on the Magisterium can be properly identified; and, through whose identification and analysis, those problems which have been visited on the Magisterium can themselves be viewed in their proper perspective.*

Specifically, the writer recognizes an obligation to suggest to all participants in the debate, on both sides of the issue, that unless a greater emphasis is placed on a treatment of the provocative and difficult concept of academic freedom, *as this is essentially related to the premise of those who have argued for the existence of "two magisteria,"* a real resolution to the ongoing debate will be delayed indefinitely.

How, then, is the logic of those who opt for two magisteria related to the framework of academic freedom?

To understand the theologians' identification of two magisteria, one must relate their intellectual jump from their right *to do research* to their questionable right *to doctrinally teach* the results of that research.

As a consequence of this leap from "to do" to "to doctrinally teach," with regard to research, it is but another short and quick step for them to substitute the concept of "authority" for the concept of "right" and, therefore, to go quite easily from the authority to do research to the authority to doctrinally teach the results of that research.

Thus, from this jump from *to do* to *to teach*, is born the "teaching authority" which these theologians have ascribed to themselves in matters that are connected with the faith and its practice.

A second "logical" conclusion follows from the first "leap": since professional competency is the prerequisite for the *doing* of research, and since only the professional theologians possess this competency, it follows that only the theologians possess the authority to teach doctrinally in matters connected with the faith.

And, thus is born the concept of a "doctrinal" teaching authority that must be distinguished from a "jurisdictional" teaching authority that is related to the bishops and the Pope.

Still a third conclusion follows from the first two intellectual "leaps": since these theologians have this doctrinal authority to teach, it follows that this "doctrinal magisterium" has also the authority to judge the value of the doctrine that is to be taught.

This leap from the right to do research to the right and authority to doctrinally teach this research, lies at the very heart of the problems that plague all of Catholic higher education today. Questions concerning the teaching of Catholic theology in the Catholic colleges and universities remain debated and unresolved, due to the introduction of a concept of professional freedom and authority that transforms the right of the theologian to do research in his field of competency to the authority and right to doctrinally teach that research to the faithful.

It is evident, therefore, that those who defend the "one magisterium" position and who address themselves to a positive statement on the teaching authority of the Church, cannot accept the theologians' premise that has sparked the debate. Nor must they grant it to the theologians.

It is evident, too, that this premise cannot be taken for granted by those who continue, under its aegis, to defend the existence of two magisteria.

It is, therefore, the writer's judgment that the subject of academic freedom, as it relates to the theologians' transfer of the "to do" to the "to teach," should serve as the framework within which the *premise* of those who defend the existence of two magisteria is *examined and tested,* and, from which the premise and conclusions of those who concern themselves with a positive statement on the magisterium, can be better understood and evaluated.

Without this delineated framework, where the spark that initiated the debate can be isolated and subjected to critical analysis, a resolution of the problems of the Magisterium will be delayed indefinitely.

Within this delineated framework, where the *premise and the claims made by the theologians can be placed in their proper perspective,* the positive statements of the "Symposium on the Magisterium: A Positive Statement," can bring about a resolution to the endlessness of the debate.

ACKNOWLEDGEMENTS*

Acknowledgement and appreciation are due to His Eminence, Cardinal Krol, and His Excellency, Bishop Maloney, for their detailed treatment of the authentic membership of the Magisterium and for their in-depth study of the authentic source of the magisterial authority; to Father Grech, of the Augustinian College in Rome, for his identification of the major problems and for his tracing of the Scriptures and Tradition for the backgrounds that have shaped the development of thought in these areas; to His Excellency, Bishop Newman, of Ireland, for his extraordinary application of the process of political socialization to the problem of the magisterium and for his application of these principles to the relationship between higher education and the magisterial authority; to Abbot McCaffrey for his treatment of the present problems of Catholic higher education and for his identification of the Magisterium as the principle of resolution; to Bishop Vaughan* for his detailed summary of the present problems that concern the Church and for his identification of a "principle of discernment" that will serve to resolve these problems; to Doctor May, of the Catholic University of America, for his in-depth treatment of the problem of the "two magisteria" and for his evaluation of the relationship between moral theology and the Magisterium; and, to His Excellency, Archbishop Whealon, of Hartford, for his outline of the pastoral and biblical aspects of the Magisterium and for his development of the historical foundations upon which the conceptualizations of our own day have been built.

Special acknowledgement is due to Monsignor John J. O'Rourke for his scholarly editing of the manuscripts.

Finally, a special acknowledgement and appreciation are due to His Eminence, Cardinal Krol, for his unstinting support of this project of the symposium.

---

*Bishop Vaughan's contribution will be included in the second printing.

19

CHAPTER ONE

"Why a Symposium on the Magisterium?"

John Cardinal Krol

Your Excellencies, Brothers and Sisters in Christ:
On behalf of the Institute of Catholic Higher Education of San Antonio and the Archdiocese of Philadelphia, I extend a cordial welcome to all, and thank you sincerely for your presence and your interest. We pray that our modest efforts may under the guidance of the Holy Spirit, contribute positively to the authentic renewal of the Church.

It is my task to attempt to answer the question: "Why this Symposium on the Magisterium of the Church?" I submit, that the Magisterium — the teaching authority of the Church — is central to many, if not most of the problems which have troubled the Church since the Second Vatican Council. What are these problems? Cardinal Danielou identified them as problems of authority, obedience and of holiness.[1] One could say the problem is one of dilution of authority and doctrine, or as Pope Paul explained:

Catholic belief is being contaminated. Ideas are appearing in the fields of exegesis and theology which have their origin in certain bold but misleading philosophical theories and which cast doubt upon or narrow down the full meaning of the truths which the Church has taught with her rightful authority. There is a pretense that religion must be adapted to the contemporary mind; the directive wisdom of the Church's teaching authority is scorned; theological inquiry is remodeled to suit the principles of historicism; the divine inspiration

21

and historical truths of Sacred Scriptures are boldly
denied: in short, God's People are being encouraged to
adopt a new, so-called "post conciliar attitude" of mind.[2]

This statement, made ten years ago, contains
the theme of many of the Pope's addresses of the past
fifteen years. Last June 20 (1977) he told a group of
French bishops that the Church needs its theologians;
that theology as a science is distinguished from any
other science in that faith is its object and its activi-
ties are wedded to the rhythm of the life of the
Church, object of vigilance of those who are its
pastors; that the "job of teachers is always complementary to that of the pastors."[3] He added:

> It is to misunderstand seriously the meaning of the
> conciliar event to take it as authority for setting up a
> so-called theological method that would permit, in the
> name of creativity and freedom of research, the interpre-
> tation to each person's taste of the scriptural text, the
> content of tradition, and setting one's self up as a judge
> of the teaching and directives of the supreme authority
> of the Church.[4]

In the same speech, commenting on the application of the rules of fundamental theology regarding
doctrinal assent to conciliar documents and statements of the Magisterium, he explained:

> But if such rules define the degree of assent due
> to each statement, none of them dispenses from suitable
> docility, and still less opens the door to unreserved
> criticism. *Respect for the Magisterium is a constitutive
> element of theological method.* And also respect for the
> People of God, who have a right not to be inconsid-
> erably troubled by adventurous hypotheses or positions,
> which it does not have the competence to judge or
> which run the risk of being simplified or manipulated
> by movements of opinion.[5]

A similar concern was expressed by the Dutch
industrialist, Antoine van den Boogard, who as
president of the Concilium Foundation, addressed
a "World Congress on the Future of the Church"
in Brussels, on September 12, 1970. He said that he

had the good or bad fortune to come into contact with theologians, who taught him much and enriched his life, but who as "an entirely special breed apart" were a disappointment to him. He faulted them for contributing to the impression "that the venerable authority of the Holy See has been replaced by the authority of many theological chairs." He added that "today the poor laymen see themselves confronted with many authorities in their own country." He compared the Magisterium to the management or direction, and the theologians to the research department of an industrial firm, saying that both must serve the one firm—the one Church. He concluded his speech with the plea: "Tell me in simple words what the Gospel and Christ mean for today, so that I can come to hear the evangelical message in a simple and intelligible way."[6]

The 1977-1978 Gallup Opinion Index on Religion in America localizes the problem for us by its report that the American "Catholic Population, young and old alike, has grown increasingly liberal in its attitude on key issues facing the Church."[7] Similarly do we find in a recent issue of *U.S. News and World Report:* "No longer do dissenting Catholics feel compelled to drop out or join another faith. Instead, most are staying in the Church to thrash out with the hierarchy such painful issues as birth control, divorce and new modes of worship."[8] In the Gallup poll in response to the question: "How important to you are your religious beliefs?" 58% of the Catholics responded "Very Important" and 32% responded "Fairly Important."[9] There is evidence, both in the Gallup Index and in pastoral experience, that there are Catholics who dissent with the authentic teaching of the Church both in theory and in their daily lives, but still profess to be members of the Catholic Church.[10]

The problems which confront the Church today are indeed serious, but by no means terminal. These problems must be viewed within the context of the long history of the Church. From its very beginnings, the Church has been troubled by tensions between faith and theology and between obedience and authority. St. Paul cautioned Timothy to stay clear of those who make a pretense of religion but mitigate its power, and who are "always learning but never able to reach a knowledge of truth" (2 Tm. 3:5-7). He also predicted: "The time will come when people will not tolerate sound doctrine, but following their own desires, will surround themselves with teachers who tickle their ears. They will stop listening to the truth and will wander off to fables" (2 Tm. 4:3-4).

God has not failed in His promise to be with His Church. In the fourth century He raised Athanasius and Hilary to defend the authentic faith against the bishops dominated by Arian Emperors. When a secularized clergy was betraying its mission in the eleventh century, Gregory VII and Peter Damian restored discipline within the Church. In the sixteenth and seventeenth centuries, when the clergy was helpless in the face of a crisis in then contemporary society, Charles Borromeo and Francis de Sales reformed the clergy and restored the Church to her missionary vitality.

From its very beginnings the Church through a succession of ages has undergone a severity of trials, endured a fury of internal disorders and survived violent oppression and persecution. The Church, ever beset, ever ailing, ever weakened by dissension and defection, ever exhausted and expiring, continues to survive and increase in vigor and in numbers. History bears eloquent witness to this irrefutable reality and provides evidence that the Church's life and power comes not from men to whom it was entrusted, but from God who founded the Church twenty centuries ago, and remains its guiding force through all the trials.

The recent Gallup Opinion Index on Religion in America reports, "The religious scene is in a state of some turmoil, with dissension within the ranks of certain denominations and sharp debate over issues." [11] While the Catholic Church is not free of such turmoil, dissension and sharp debate, the same Gallup Index under the subtitle "Good News for Catholics" reports that the latest surveys offer findings which are encouraging; thus: "Today, a higher proportion of the adult population (18 and older) are Catholics.... The proportion of young adult (18-29) Catholics is higher than the proportion of Protestants.... An upturn in attendance at Mass is noted among the nation's youngest Catholic adults (18-29).... In a similar vein, the proportion of Catholics who give Pope Paul VI a 'highly favorable' rating has increased since 1976 from 25 percent to 37 percent." This is a 50% increase in one year. [12] At the same time, an overall favorable view of Pope Paul VI increased from 61% to 76%. [13]

In summary, the Catholic Church is certainly beset with serious problems. But the Church has never in its history been problem-free. The Church is a divinely founded and divinely guided assembly of human beings — of sinners. Even with such problems, the Church in the United States shows clear evidence of vigor and vitality. However, we cannot be complacent. We cannot assume that problems will evaporate — without human prayer and effort. God is present in His Church. He directs and guides it. But He uses human instruments. Those to whom He entrusted the Church must be relentless in their efforts to purify it, to renew and reform it. That is why we assemble in this Symposium, to highlight the problems by discussion, by the presentation of the truth and by pointing out errors. Pope St. Felix III (483-492) stated: "Not to oppose error is to approve it and truth which is not defended is suppressed." [14]

Purpose of Vatican Council II:

It seems incredible that the Church today is experiencing problems on the subject of its teaching authority. In his opening speech to the Second Vatican Council, Pope John XXIII declared that he convoked the Council for the purpose of reaffirming again the teaching authority of the Church: *"ut iterum Magisterium Ecclesiasticum, numquam deficiens et ad finem usque temporum perseverans, affirmaretur."* [15] He added: "The *greatest concern* of the Ecumenical Council is this: that the sacred deposit of Christian doctrine should be guarded and taught more efficaciously." [16]

A month after the conclusion of the Council, Pope Paul VI said on January 12, 1966: "The Council is a great act of the Magisterium of the Church, and anyone who adheres to the Council is, by that very fact, recognizing and honoring the Magisterium of the Church." [17]

During the second session of the Council on November 4, 1964, Pope Paul had deemed it necessary to deplore the attacks on the Church and its authority. [18] After the third session on July 7, 1965, he had complained: "A spirit of criticism and even indocility and rebellion is calling into question sacrosanct norms for Christian life, for the conduct of clerics, for religious perfection,... conscience is deprived of the light of moral precepts, the notion of sin is changed, obedience is impugned and its constitutional function in the ordering of the ecclesial community is contested." [19]

On July 28, 1965, Pope Paul took issue with those who take the problems raised by the Council and the discussions it generates "as an occasion for stirring up a spirit of discontent and of radical reformism in themselves and in others." He said: "This happens in both the doctrinal and disciplinary fields, as if the Council were a timely occasion for challenging dogmas and laws that the Church has inscribed in the tables of her own fidelity to Christ the Lord; and as if it were authorizing every private individual to pass judgments stripping the patrimony of the Church of all things acquired as a result of its long history and well-substantiated experience in the course of the centuries." The Pope added: "In the same way, we won't describe as good interpreters of orthodoxy those who are suspicious of the Council's decisions and reserve to themselves the right to accept only the ones they judge to be valid, as if it were legitimate to question the Council's authority.... There isn't enough thought given to the fact that when the Church gives lessons as a Teacher, then everyone has to become a pupil...." [20]

After the close of the Council, Pope Paul in his Christmas message to the Cardinals, insisted on December 23, 1965,

> The Council has not inaugurated a period of dogmatic and moral uncertainty, or of disciplinary indifference, or superficial religious irenicism or of organizational weakening. [21]

On January 12, 1966, the Holy Father explained that the authority of the Council was quite clear from the declaration issued on March 6, 1964, and repeated on November 16, 1964. [22] He explained: "In view of the pastoral nature of the Council, it avoided any extraordinary statement of dogmas that would be endowed with the note of infallibility, but it still provided its teaching with the authority of the supreme ordinary Magisterium, which is so obviously official, it has to be accepted with the docility and sincerity by all the faithful." [23]

The following month, February 21, 1966, Pope Paul talked about the great amount of restlessness, criticisms, intolerance and disobedience. He said: "Authority in the Church is something willed by Christ. Anyone who thinks that there will have to be a complete and total revision of Church discipline and who maintains that canonical legislation is outdated and anachronistic is not on the right road. He is hurting the Church by tearing apart its spiritual and social fabric, and he is hurting himself by depriving himself of the merit of spontaneous, filial and manly docility and of the strength and comfort that comes from humility, good example, and trust."[24]

Returning to the question "Why a Symposium on the Magisterium?" we can say that Pope John's purpose in convoking the Council—to reaffirm the Magisterium of the Church—was achieved admirably in the conciliar documents. Regrettably, some regarded the openness of the conciliar discussions as an invitation to challenge the teachings of the Council and of the Church. The number of those challenging was not significant and the merits of their challenge were not compelling. However, since they represented a controversial element, they made good copy, and their voices and impact were magnified by media headlines. They became the favorites of reporters who normally look for the atypical and anormal to write interesting stories.

It was my privilege to have been a member of a preparatory Commission of the Council, an undersecretary of the Vatican Council, a member of the Coordinating or Steering Committee of the Council, and for a year following the Council to have served on the Committee for Interpretation and Implementation. I serve on the Commission for the Revision of the Code of Canon Law, and I am a member of the Sacred Congregation for the Doctrine of the Faith. Frankly, I have been scandalized and shocked by the reaction of some of our "experts" to statements and instructions issuing from the Holy See. I have heard criticism and even sweeping condemnations of such instructions. I know for a fact that some of the criticism and condemnation came from persons who had not even read or seen the documents.

You know, as well as I, that in some circles more attention is paid to dissent than to assent, and non-infallible teaching is equated with fallible teaching and as something a person is free to reject. You have heard the strident criticism of the "institutional" or "official" Church, as if Christ had instituted more than one Church. You have heard the ministerial priesthood identified with clerical usurpation. You have read of the naive attempt to wed the disjunctive beliefs of Christianity and Marxism, under a banner of the white robe of baptism and the red flag of revolution. You have heard of the "private affair" syndrome which values personal beliefs above the authentic teaching of the Church.

Again the question, "Why this Symposium on the Magisterium?" This Symposium is certainly not an attack on theologians. The Church has need of theologians. Theologians—including a past president of the Catholic Theological Society of America—are presenting the papers. We hope by this Symposium to eliminate at least some of the confusion that has disturbed the Church and the People of God.

We fervently hope and pray that out of this Symposium there will issue a positive statement in clear and simple words:

that Jesus was a teacher—an unusual one who taught with authority;

that Jesus was "a prophet powerful in word and deed in the eyes of God and all the people";

that Jesus came to offer His sacrifice of expiation and to sanctify us with His Spirit;

that Jesus founded a new teaching organization which He called His Church;

that Jesus founded a new teaching tradition and established a new teaching authority;

that Jesus sent His disciples to teach and baptize men of all nations, teaching them to observe all His Commandments;

that the task of authentically interpreting the Word of God, whether written or in the form of tradition, has been entrusted exclusively to the living teaching office of the Church, whose authority is exercised in the name of Jesus Christ;[25]

that the function of the theologian "is to bring to the knowledge of the Christian community, and particularly of the Magisterium, the fruit of its research so that, through the doctrine taught by the ecclesiastical hierarchy, they become a light for all Christian People";[26]

that the People of God has particular need of the intervention and assistance of the Magisterium when internal disagreements arise and spread concerning a doctrine that must be believed or held, lest it lose communion of the faith in the one Body of the Lord (cf. Eph. 4:4-5).[27]

Footnotes

1. See *Documentation Catholique* 66 (1969) 881.
2. Apostolic Exhortation *Petrum et Paulum*, *Acta Apostolicae Sedis* 59 (1967) 198.
3. *Acta Apostolicae Sedis* 69 (1977) 588.
4. *Acta Apostolicae Sedis* 69 (1977) 589.
5. *Acta Apostolicae Sedis* 69 (1977) 589. Emphasis added.
6. *Documentary Service, U.S. Catholic Conference* press release dated September 18, 1970. See *Ephemerides Theologicae Lovanienses* 47 (1971) 238 for some reaction.
7. G. Gallup, *Religion in America 1977-78* (Princeton, 1977) 6.
8. "Catholicism: A New Vitality Emerging Out of Ferment," *U.S. News & World Report* 82, 14 (April 11, 1977) 63.
9. Gallup, *Religion in America 1977-78*, 9.
10. See, e.g., Gallup poll for August 7, 1977.
11. Gallup, *Religion in America 1977-78*, 1.
12. Gallup, *Religion in America 1977-78*, 5f.
13. NC News Service release of October 25, 1977.
14. Migne, *Patrologia Latina* Vol. 58, 897.
15. *Acta Apostolicae Sedis* 54 (1962) 786. In translation, "to assert once again the magisterium, which is unfailing and perdures to the end of time."
16. *Acta Apostolicae Sedis* 54 (1962) 790.
17. *The Pope Speaks* 11 (1966) 153.

18. *The Pope Speaks* 10 (1965/66) 116-119.

19. *The Pope Speaks* 10 (1965/66) 346.

20. *The Pope Speaks* 10 (1965/66) 351.

21. *Acta Apostolicae Sedis* 58 (1966) 81f.

22. *Acta Apostolicae Sedis* 57 (1965) 72-75. See *The Pope Speaks* 10 (1965/66) 400ff.

23. *The Pope Speaks* 11 (1966) 154.

24. *Acta Apostolicae Sedis* 58 (1966) 228.

25. Vatican Council II, Constitution *Dei Verbum* on Divine Revelation n. 10.

26. Pope Paul VI to the International Theological Congress on October 1, 1966; *Acta Apostolicae Sedis* 58 (1966) 291.

27. Cf. Paul VI, Encyclical *Mysterium Fidei*, *Acta Apostolicae Sedis* 57 (1965) 755f.

CHAPTER TWO

The Magisterium in Scripture and Tradition

Very Rev. Prospero M. Grech

It is evident that the title of this lecture is too broad to be dealt with in its entirety. We shall have to limit it. On the other hand I do not think that I have been invited to repeat what can be found in any good theological textbook, and adduce all the arguments from scripture and tradition that the Pope and bishops have the right and duty to exercise teaching authority in the Church. I am speaking to Catholics who are so because they accept the authority of both Vatican I and II. These two councils leave no doubt whatsoever about this point. If anyone feels otherwise he had better start looking for some more harmless brand of Christianity. The principal paragraph in Vatican II concerning the hierarchy is:

"Among the principal duties of bishops, the preaching of the gospel occupies an eminent place. For bishops are preachers of the faith who lead new disciples to Christ. They are authentic teachers, that is, teachers endowed with the authority of Christ, who preach to the people committed to them the faith they must believe and put into practice. By the light of the Holy Spirit, they make that faith clear, bringing forth from the treasury of revelation new things and old (cf. Mt. 13:52), making faith bear fruit and vigilantly warding off any errors which threaten their flock (cf. 2 Tm. 4:1-4).

"Bishops, teaching in communion with the Roman Pontiff, are to be respected by all as witnesses to divine and Catholic truth. In matters of faith and morals, the bishops speak in the name of Christ and the faithful are to accept their teaching and adhere to it with a religious assent of soul. This religious submission of will and of mind must be shown in a special way to the authentic teaching authority of the Roman Pontiff, even when he is not speaking ex cathedra. That is, it must be shown in such a way that his supreme magisterium is acknowledged with reverence, the judgments made by him are sincerely adhered to, according to his manifest mind and will. His mind and will in the matter may be known chiefly either from the character of the documents, from his frequent repetition of the same doctrine, or from his manner of speaking.

"Although the individual bishops do not enjoy the prerogative of infallibility, they can nevertheless proclaim Christ's doctrine infallibly. This is so, even when they are dispersed around the world, provided that while maintaining the bond of unity among themselves and with Peter's successor, and while teaching authentically on a matter of faith or morals, they concur in a single viewpoint as the one which must be held conclusively. This authority is even more clearly verified when, gathered together in an ecumenical council, they are teachers and judges of faith and morals for the universal Church. Their definitions must then be adhered to with the submission of faith.

"This infallibility with which the divine Redeemer willed His Church to be endowed in defining a doctrine of faith and morals extends as far as extends the deposit of divine revelation, which must be religiously guarded and faithfully expounded. This is the infallibility which the Roman Pontiff, the head of the college of bishops, enjoys in virtue of his office, when, as the supreme shepherd and teacher of all the faithful, who confirms his brethren in their faith (cf. Lk. 22:32), he proclaims by a definitive act some doctrine of faith or morals. Therefore his definitions, of themselves, and not from the consent of the Church, are justly styled irreformable, for they are pronounced with the assistance of the Holy Spirit, an assistance promised to him in blessed Peter. Therefore they need no approval of others, nor do they allow an appeal to any other judgment. For then the Roman Pontiff is not pronouncing judgment as a private person. Rather, as the supreme teacher of the universal Church, as one in whom the charism of the infallibility of the Church herself is individually present, he is expounding or defending a doctrine of Catholic faith.

"The infallibility promised to the Church resides also in the body of bishops when that body exercises supreme teaching authority with the successor of Peter. To the resultant definitions the assent of the Church can never be wanting, on account of the activity of that same Holy Spirit, whereby the whole flock of Christ is preserved and progresses in unity of faith.

"But when either the Roman Pontiff or the body of bishops together with him defines a judgment, they pronounce it in accord with revelation itself. All are obliged to maintain and be ruled by this revelation, which, as written or preserved by tradition, is transmitted in its entirety through the legitimate succession of bishops and especially through the care of the Roman Pontiff himself.

"Under the guiding light of the Spirit of truth, revelation is thus religiously preserved and faithfully expounded in the Church. The Roman Pontiff and the bishops, in view of their office and of the importance of the matter, strive painstakingly and by appropriate means to inquire properly into that revelation and to give apt expression to its contents. But they do not allow that there could be any new public revelation pertaining to the divine deposit of faith" (L.G. 25).

So far the doctrine of Vatican II on the magisterial authority of the bishops and the Supreme Pontiff. As you see, the real problem does not reside in the fact that the pastors of the Church possess this authority but rather in the way it is to be exercised. It is my purpose in the present paper to analyze the ecclesial situation which has arisen after the Vatican Council, to try to discern some emerging patterns of behavior which cause difficulties in the relationships between the teaching authorities and the faithful, subsequently to look for analogous patterns in New Testament Christianity and in the Church of the second century, and then come back to the present to see in what way the situational difficulties of the very first Christians can help both the faithful and the hierarchy today to strike an equilibrium which will safeguard the unity of love and faith. This, I hope, will both set the tone and provide the context of subsequent papers and discussions in the symposium.

It is undeniable that the last fifteen years have witnessed a veritable revolution within the Church. Mark you, there has been an ideological revolution outside the Church as well. The teen-age upheaval has burst many traditional patterns of thought and life, and it was inevitable that the general atmosphere outside the Church should also influence life within. We are still full of tensions. There are those who yearn for the good old days of Pius XII and others who look forward to Vatican III. The truth is that the Church has not yet fully absorbed Vatican II although there are obvious signs that we are moving towards an equilibrium. We are very much like Abraham who, at the command of the Lord, has left his home and country to move towards a new promised land but can only hail it from afar.

Let us examine the emerging patterns which characterize the present-day Church, distinguish positive values and dangers and try to pin-point the place of authority and magisterium in their guidance. We shall do well to begin with the life of prayer in the Church. The new liturgy and the use of the vernacular have certainly broadened the set forms of pre-conciliar days and rendered more easy the participation of the faithful in the Eucharistic sacrifice. Some may feel a little homesick for the old Latin liturgy, but others are not content with the broadening of the boundaries, and run away with their newly gained liberty often into realms of fantasy. The charismatic groups which have sprung up all over the world bear witness that people want to pray more, not less; that they want their prayer to be more spontaneous and to let the Spirit guide their words wherever He will. As far as recognizing the tree by its fruit is concerned we cannot deny that Christian living has been enriched by this form of prayer. The limits are overstepped when spontaneity is set against official prayer, and uninhibited feeling overpowers reason so that it is hard to discern where the Spirit stops and neurosis begins.

The same pattern of tension between formalism and caprice is to be observed in moral behavior. Having set aside the casuistry of our old moral theology textbooks we enjoy now a newly-found liberty of action which is based on Gospel principles, and which, while continuing along the lines of traditional Catholic ethics, gives broader scope to individual responsibility. Even here, though, alongside old-guard stiffness we find theologians and laity who lend a more generous ear to Freud than to Paul, to Marx than to Christ. This is nowhere more obvious than in the realm of sexual ethics.

But even as regards authority we are in no better position. Gone is the notion that a superior is there to impose his will on his subjects. Thank God, new ways of reasoning consider authority as a ministry, a service to the community. Dialogue between pastor and laity, parents and children and between superiors and religious gives more freedom of movement to both parties, but it is easy for dialogue to degenerate into contestation, let alone the fact that the word obedience has almost disappeared from our vocabulary.

Post-conciliar theology is perhaps the area which causes most concern to both hierarchy and laity. It is characterized by two key-words: hermeneutics and inculturation. We all remember how our old theology textbooks proceeded: the enunciation of a thesis taken from the text of a council, then the enumeration of the "adversaries," proof from scripture, proof from the Fathers, arguments from reason and confutation of heretics. The insistence of the Council on the primacy of biblical theology with pastoral and liturgical intents, the progress of exegesis and the challenge of an agnostic world has altered the view-point of contemporary courses in our seminaries. Many people felt, however, that even with biblical theology the language it uses cannot be adequately understood by people living in the twentieth Century who take a completely different view of life than that prevalent at the time of the New Testament authors and the Fathers. It is necessary to "translate," in the sense of to "transfer," this language into modern expression accommodated to mentalities, varying in time and place, whose outlook is formed by sundry philosophies and scientific theories. Hence diverse theologies have sprung up: Political Theology, Kerygmatic Theology, Theologies of Liberation, Theology of Hope, and various Christologies. Some find this pluralism truly bewildering and scrap all the "isms" into the wastepaper basket.

A calmer study of the problem, however, reveals that innumerable areas of our ecclesial and private lives as well as many problems facing the modern world have been illuminated by these present trends in theology. Nevertheless it is very difficult to see how some demythologizing theories can be reconciled with the supernatural or how scientific inculturation does not surrender biblical principles to anthropology and psychology. Is there any sense in a plurality of theologies? Which is the principle of unity that keeps them together? Which are the limits between orthodoxy and error? Should we still speak at all about orthodoxy? How can a poor bishop keep up with all these new doctrines when even the Congregation of the Faith itself is sometimes at a loss?

Another characteristic of the post-conciliar Church is the awareness of social responsibility. Some of the theologies just mentioned, especially political theology and the theology of liberation spring from unpleasant social and political situations in South America and in the Third World. Here in the United States there is the color problem, in Italy the problem of collaborating with the Marxists. Would it not be easier to devote ourselves entirely to prayer and leave other problems to the politicians? Others, on the contrary, want only social action with the minimum of unction. Two extremes: where lies the happy balance?

All the movements we have reviewed have one common pattern: traditionalism on one extreme, progressive exaggerations on the other, and a healthy middle line; in other words, those who move too fast, those who do not want to move at all, and those who move with prudence. This is a static picture. Expressed dynamically in terms of history, we have a trajectory which begins with the Council, moves along the pathways of ecclesial life and flies off at a tangent at some point or other. The many movements follow several intersecting trajectories which can coexist in a happy pluralism within the Church, all contributing in one way or another to Christian living, but they leave the Church when they escape the control of an inner tension which keeps them Catholic. What is this factor which keeps them within ecclesial limits? We have spoken about pluralism in unity, but is it right to have conflicting parties within the Church? Is it correct for some groups to stop the clock and remain immobile while others move ahead? Can we subscribe to Archbishop Lefèbvre's position which wants to go back to Pius X or to that of certain theologians who fly onwards regardless of tradition and orthodoxy? Where lies the function of the Magisterium in this complex situation? This is our problem, and we shall try to find the answer in similar patterns within the New Testament and in the second century.

Let us begin with the charismatic trajectory. When the Old Testament prophets wanted to characterize the essence of the eschatological age they foretold an extraordinary outpouring of the Spirit. Joel 2 is quoted at length by Peter in his Pentecostal speech (Acts 2:17-21), and we have two parallel passages which are often quoted or referred to in the New Testament: Jeremiah 31:31ff. and Ezekiel 36:26. Both prophecies describe the change of heart of the New Israel but Ezekiel emphasizes the gift of the Spirit: "A new heart I will give you, and a new spirit I will put within you.... I will put my spirit within you, and cause you to walk in my statutes." This prophecy was accomplished on the day of Pentecost, and its illustration runs through the Acts of the Apostles like a golden thread, so that we can summarize Luke's theology on the subject in the words: Where the Spirit manifests itself there is eschatological salvation. It does so in prayer meetings of Christians through the gift of tongues and prophecy, the gifts of healing and heart reading. However, very

early we witness some confusion in the church of
Corinth, and the Apostle Paul has to intervene
authoritatively to establish some order (1 Cor.
12), reminding the Corinthians that the supreme gifts of
the Spirit, which they should all aim at, are faith,
hope and, especially, charity (1 Cor. 13). Apostolic
authority, therefore, is over and above charismatic
manifestation. On the other hand Paul has no wish to
extinguish the Spirit (1 Thes. 5:19). He himself is
a charismatic insofar as he is a Christian, but when
he announces the Word of God he does so through
the sword of the Spirit (Eph. 6:17). The response to
Apostolic preaching is the act of faith, which is
also produced by the Spirit. Confessions of faith
such, as "Jesus is Lord" are charismatic manifesta-
tions, but even these are sometimes subject to
illusion and have to be corrected by the Apostle.
In Corinth, it seems, some people, appealing to the
Spirit, were casting curses on the earthly Jesus
in contrast to the Risen Christ, and Paul warns them
that no one can say "Cursed be Jesus" in the Spirit
(1 Cor. 12:3). Even when the faithful appeal to
angelic revelations against Apostolic teaching Paul
answers: "For even if we, or an angel from heaven,
should preach to you a gospel contrary to that which
we preached to you, let him be accursed" (Gal. 1:8).
Paul, therefore, recognizes and acknowledges the
positive power of the Spirit within the communities
but harnasses it to defend it from deception, and
sets its limit within the established doctrine of
Apostolic preaching.

St. John also makes use of the charismatic
potentialities of his community. In his Gospel
he says that the new community will be taught by
God (6:45), while in 14:26 he narrows his saying with
reference to the Spirit who will teach the believers
everything and render witness to Christ (15:26).
In John's first letter, in fact, the Apostle appeals
to this very unction of the Spirit within the hearts

of the faithful to defend them against error: the teachers of false doctrines "went out from us, but they were not of us; for if they had been of us they would have continued with us; but they went out, that it might be plain that they all are not of us. But you have been anointed by the Holy One, and you all know" (1 Jn. 2:19f.). A dialogue exists between the Apostle and the *sensus fidei* of the faithful, produced by the Spirit of God, which enables the Church to distinguish right doctrine from error.

The Pastoral Epistles attribute the preservation of the doctrine entrusted to Timothy to the Spirit: "Guard the truth, which has been entrusted to you by the Holy Spirit who dwells within us" (1 Tm. 1:14).

Charismatic phenomena continued well into the second Century, and many are the beautiful witnesses of martyrs before their tribunals. They fell into disrepute, however, with the rise of the Montanist movement. Montanus and his prophetess Maximilla claimed for themselves charismatic authority to criticize the softer line the Church was taking with penitents. Tertullian himself was deceived by them.[2] Their exaggerations caused them to be condemned by the Asiatic bishops late in the second Century.[3] From then onwards all forms of Pentecostalism were immediately suspect, which is a pity. But as these forms of enthusiasm are so difficult to harnass and keep within the limits of faith, hope and charity the Church preferred to live without them rather than be in constant peril of seeing its unity and teaching threatened. The recent rebirth within the Catholic Church of charismatic groups might be a reminder that the Spirit is still operative within the hearts of the faithful even in an overt fashion, but if this movement does not want to fly off at a tangent like the Montanists it will have to create a very close dialogue with the rest of the faithful and particularly with the teaching authority.

The second post-conciliar problem we mentioned was the use of a newly-gained liberty. Nowhere can this pattern be studied any better than in the New Testament. As you all know the very first converts to Christianity were Jewish-Christians. They believed in Jesus as the Christ but continued their Jewish way of life, circumcising their children and observing the Law of Moses. When the first converts from paganism were admitted into the Church a big controversy arose as to whether these should only be baptized and accept the faith or else whether they too should be circumcised and observe the Mosaic Law. In a council in Jerusalem (Acts 15) it was decided that this was not necessary. Speaking at this meeting Peter says: "Now why do you make trial of God by putting a yoke upon the neck of the disciples which neither our fathers nor we have been able to bear? But we believe that we shall be saved through the grace of the Lord Jesus Christ, just as they will" (vv. 10:11). Peter therefore asserts that not only the gentiles were freed from the Law but also the Jewish converts themselves. It is grace that saves, not the works of the Law. We all know how St. Paul made himself the herald of this message of freedom. In fact he became its official theologian. His letters to the Romans and to the Galatians about justification by faith were received with a sigh of relief not only by gentile Christians but also by many ex-Jews themselves. Such a message, however, was open to gross misinterpretation as libertinism, and Paul himself was well aware of this: "What shall we say then? Are we to continue in sin that grace may abound? By no means! How can you who died to sin still live in it?" (Rom. 6:1f.) His ethical teaching and exhortations in the second part of the epistle are very severe. In chapter 7 and 8 of Romans he explains quite clearly what he means by liberty. Man is a slave to his passions and egoism. The Mosaic Law tells him what is to be done but does not help

him do it; it remains a dead letter. Man is freed from
the slavery of sin by the greater power which is given
him by the Holy Spirit. He is now truly free, free to
obey and to do good in response to God's call, not to
live degernerately. Degenerate Christians do not
inherit the kingdom of God (1 Cor. 6:9-11). In spite
of these warnings the Pauline doctrine of freedom
was used by some as an excuse for licenciousness
(1 Cor. 6:12ff.) even within the Corinthian community.
From these groups of antinomians arose, and later
the Gnostics topped up the measure by teaching utter
sexual unrestraint. All this went under the name of
Paul. The heretic Marcion in the second Century
went so far as to accept only ten letters of Paul
as canonical from the whole of the New Testament,
and Luke, of course, who is Pauline, thus opposing
the good God of love of the New Testament to "the
wicked God" of the Old. Paul himself must have
turned in his grave when such doctrines were pro-
pounded in his name and must have been thankful
to St. Polycarp who addressed Marcion as "The first-
born of Satan"![4] Here, therefore, is a trajectory which
leads from the purest doctrine of grace and works,
through misinterpretation, to heresy. Alongside this
we have another counter-trajectory which balances
Paul and tries to correct misinterpretation. We refer
to the epistle of James and to the Gospel of Matthew.
James puts it quite bluntly: "Show me your faith
apart from your works, and I by my works shall
show you my faith...even the demons believe—and
shudder" (2:18f.). There is no contradiction between
Paul and James, only opposite but reconcilable points
of view. In fact the happy medium was struck by the
author of the Gospel of Matthew who lived in a
Jewish-Christian community open to pagans but with
very definite ideas about church order and morality.
The Sermon on the Mount becomes the new law of
the new Israel. The Mosaic law is out of fashion
not because it is too difficult but because it does not

reach up to the standards of the more radical ethics of love Even Matthew, unfortunately, in spite of his equilibrium, was not accepted by all. A fringe of Jewish Christians would not rise to the occasion and enjoy its newly gained liberty. They even found the profession of Jesus as Son of God too much for them, and, again in the second Century, fell out of the Church Universal. We have groups falling out, therefore, either because they run too far ahead of their appointed teachers or because they lag far behind, in spite of the fact that within the Church itself there are different emphases which suit all temperaments.

Some years after Paul's death, in the ever turbulent city of Corinth, a group of younger believers started contesting their presbyter/bishops. They received a sharp rap on the knuckles from none other than the bishop of Rome, Clement I, successor of Peter, who not only exercises authority in a community which is not his own, but justifies such an action theoretically with the words: "The Apostles received the gospel for us from the Lord Jesus Christ. Jesus the Christ was sent from God...the Apostles received their instructions.... They preached in country and town, and appointed their first-fruits, after testing them by the Spirit, to be bishops and deacons of those who were going to believe." [5] Together with the gospel of liberty, therefore, we find in the very earliest Church, authority used in the service of order, and order in the service of love.

We now come to a more important point. We mentioned above the role of hermeneutics and inculturation in present-day theology. Can we find any examples of this process in the first centuries? Were they positive contributions? How did the teaching authorities of the Church behave? Christology provides us with an excellent illustration. When the Apostles preached the Risen Christ immediately after Pentecost they did so in Palestine,

speaking to Jews in their own language, Aramaic.
They used Jewish thought patterns to express their
new experience of Christ and the Spirit, insisting
that Jesus was the expected Messiah. After some
time the gospel had to be preached outside Palestine
to both Greek-speaking Jews and to gentiles. As a
Greek translation of the bible, the Septuagint, had
already been in use for two centuries the transition
was not difficult, but many Greek terms used in a
biblical context had quite a different meaning in
the ears of a gentile. The word Messiah, *Christos*,
Anointed, was meaningless to a Greek. So in the
gentile mission Christos soon became the proper
name, almost the surname, of Jesus. Jesus the Christ
became Jesus Christ. His new title was *Kyrios*, Lord.
But *Kyrios* was used in the Septuagint to denote
God, and it had strong connotations of divinity in
the pagan world too. Son of God was equivalent to
Messiah in late Judaism, at the most understood
as adopted sonship. In the pagan world Son of God
had a more ontological meaning. This does not mean
that Christ was deified because of an accidental
change of language, the opposite is true. The experience of the power of the Risen Christ, which
could not be explained unless He were, in some way,
God, could not continue to subsist in the old wine-
skins of Aramaic. The new language expressed
the experience more adequately. And when emperors
started calling themselves *sōtēr*, savior, and *dominus*
and *deus noster* — Our Lord and God — as in the case
of Domitian, the Christians countered this confession
with an application to Christ, our Savior, our Lord
and God, not, however, in the sense in which the
emperor used it, but in the sense in which Yahweh
was savior, Lord and God, as revealed by the manifestation of the Holy Spirit. Christology, therefore,
progressed until it reached unsuspected heights
in John who discovered the term *Logos*, the Word,
and applied it to the pre-existent Lord. Many Pal-

estinian Christians, who thought that their Greek-speaking brethren were going too far, stuck to their old adoptionist Christology and lagged behind, content with professing Jesus as the Messiah but not as Son of God. These were the predecessors of the Arians. The Catholic Church moved forward, making use, in post-New Testament times, of Greek philosophy to polish its concepts, and arrived at the Council of Nicea where Christ was declared *homoousios*, of the same nature, as the Father, and Arius was condemned.[6] Here we find both hermeneutics and inculturation, meaning the translation of concepts and experiences not merely into another tongue but into another language or way of speaking, adapting it to the culture of those to whom it is preached. Of course there are dangers in this process of translation and adaptation, and the rise of the Gnostic heresy in the second Century is the best illustration. Instead of using philosophy to illustrate and express the Christian faith, the Gnostics wanted to adapt the Christian faith to philosophy, to render it more palatable to those outside. Now in current Greek thought, especially in Plato, matter was despised in favor of spirit; the body was only the prison of the soul. Hence a bodily resurrection is both impossible and meaningless, so is the incarnation of God in a human body and the subsequent doctrine of eating the body of Christ in the Eucharist. We encounter the first difficulties among gnosticising Christians in Corinth who denied the resurrection of the body and logically the true resurrection of Christ. Paul counters them not with philosophical arguments in 1 Corinthians 15 but with an appeal to direct witness of the fact of the resurrection. The mystery of Christ has precedence over philosophy, where the two are in conflict philosophy must give way. The Incarnation was impugnate for the same reasons, by the docetists, who taught that Christ's body was only an apparent body not a real one, so was his death on the cross, and so is the Eucharist. Ignatius of Antioch, writing about the year 110, refers to those "who abstain from the Eucharist and from prayer, because they do not confess that the Eucharist is the flesh of our Savior Jesus Christ, flesh which suffered for our sins and which the Father, in his goodness, raised up again." [7] John the Apostle had written his Gospel a few years earlier, and obviously he had encountered the same objections. He countered these with the brief account of the conversation between Jesus and the unbelieving disciples after the Eucharistic sermon in chapter 6: "Many of his disciples, when they heard it, said, 'This is a hard saying, who can listen to it?'... After this many of his disciples drew back and no longer went about with him. Jesus said to the twelve, 'Will you also go away?' Simon Peter answered him, 'Lord, to whom shall we go? You have the words of eternal life; and we have believed, and have come to know that you are the Holy One of God'" (vv. 60-69). Jesus and John are uncompromising in their firmness. There is a limit even to the hermeneutics when the essence of the faith is in danger of being compromised.

Gnosticism developed into a quite complicated system, or rather into complicated systems, as the century progressed. It became more and more of a theosophy rather than a philosophy or a theology, and many were its victims. Its greatest adversary was St. Irenaeus. This great theologian is no mere repeater of formulas. He is one of the most important milestones on the way to Nicea. His hermeneutics can be summarized in his own words: "That in which we have faith is a firm system directed to the salvation of men, and, since it has been received by the Church, we guard it. Constantly it has its youth renewed by the Spirit of God, as if it were some precious deposit in some excellent vessel; and it causes the vessel containing it also to be rejuvenated."[8] He himself rejuvenated both theology and the Church of the late second century. When expounding Catholic doctrine both for pastoral purposes and as apologetic, his main witness is scripture, of course, but as not all his adversaries admitted the same canon as himself he developed the principle of tradition, and, most especially, the tradition of the Roman Church. We quote the well known text from *Adversus Haereses* 3, 3, 2: "But since it would be too long to enumerate in such a volume as this the successions of all the churches, we shall confound all those who, in whatever manner, whether through self-satisfaction or vainglory, or through blindness and wicked opinion, assemble other than where it is proper, by pointing out here the successions of the bishops of the greatest and most ancient church known to all, founded and organized at Rome by the two most glorious apostles, Peter and Paul, that church which has the tradition and the faith which comes down to us after having been announced to men by the Apostles. For with this church, because of its superior origin, all churches must agree, that is, all the faithful in the whole world; and it is in her that the faithful everywhere have maintained the Apostolic Tradition."

The doctrine maintained by the Roman Church, therefore, became the yardstick of orthodoxy all over the world, and this because of its preeminence and because of its descent from Peter and Paul. The text of Irenaeus is basic for our understanding of the teaching authority of the Bishop of Rome. This Church Father extends the principle of unity in doctrine to the bishops as well: "It is necessary to obey those who are the presbyters of the Church, those who, as we have shown, have succession from the Apostles; those who have received, with the succession of the episcopate, the sure charism of truth according to the good pleasure of the Father.

But the rest, who have no part in the primitive succession and assemble wheresoever they will, must
be held in suspicion." [9]

Irenaeus also suggests to us the limits of hermeneutics. He himself, we said, contributes to
rejuvenate theology in his own time, but one can see
that his theology is thoroughly biblical and thoroughly
Greek. Whereas the Gnostics and others had their
focal point in a philosophy outside Christianity
and explained the faith according to this philosophy,
the great theologians of the patristic era maintained
their focal point within the faith as they received
it from tradition and used philosophy to broaden
its language and adapt it to pastoral or apologetic
needs. This made all the difference between heresy
and orthodoxy, and, as we have seen in the case of
the Jewish Christians, some could even fall away from
orthodoxy by sticking to repetitive formulas and
refusing to live forwards with the Church.

Does the magisterium extend to social matters?
It is obvious that in the first two centuries the Church
could not change the world it was living in. In the
New Testament, however, we find three sayings
which subsequently revolutionized the whole course
of Christian society: the blessing of the poor and meek
in the Sermon on the Mount; Paul's statement that
"There is neither Jew nor Greek, there is neither
slave nor free, there is neither male nor female;
for you are all one in Christ Jesus" (Gal. 3:28); and
James' taunt against the injustices of the rich which
sounds very much like a Marxist manifesto, though
it is far from being so (Jas. 5:1-6). The first Christians sold their superfluous goods and put them in
common. All this provoked a series of sayings among
the Holy Fathers which culminated in a veritable
sociology of riches in John Chrysostom, Ambrose,
Basil and Leo, sayings which found their place in
Pope Paul VI's encyclical *Populorum Progressio*[10]

and his Apostolic Letter *Octogesima Adveniens.*"[11]
Thus the Church becomes Christ's witness to the
world in her message of hope to suffering mankind.
But it takes its stance away from the world insofar as the latter is the enemy of the Kingdom of God.
The book of the Apocalypse is the best illustration
of the Christian prophetic interpretation of history,
a view brought to perfection in St. Augustine's
City of God.

Let us now try to draw some general conclusions
as regards the modern role of the teaching authority
of the Church, whether it be the Pope or the bishops.
It is evident from what we said that this role does
not exhaust itself in launching anathemas against
heretics, although the magisterium would fail in
its duty if it did not do so when the occasion requires
it. The role of the magisterium is more positive, pastoral and prophetic. Pastors should, first of all,
acknowledge that the Spirit of God is at work within
the community of the faithful. Their role, or their
specific gift, is that of the discernment of spirits, to
distinguish what comes from the Spirit of God to
keep the community on the move in its role of witness
to Christ, and what comes from the Evil One. The
thumb rule is given by Paul: "Now the works of the
flesh are plain: immorality, impurity, licenciousness,
idolatry, sorcery, enmity, strife, jealousy, anger,
selfishness, dissension, party spirit, envy, drunken-
ness, carousing, and the like.... But the fruit of the
Spirit is love, joy, peace, patience, kindness, goodness, faithfulness, gentleness, self-control; against
such there is no law" (Gal. 5:19-23).

In matters of doctrine the bishop is the custodian
of the inherited professions of faith, which, throughout the centuries, have been the Spirit's and the
Church's response to the apostolic kerygma. Tradition is not repetition, we have seen that development itself is part and parcel of tradition, and that

development can follow several tracks. The pastor must watch over these trajectories of thought to discern whether they are still within the magnetic field of the internal cohesion of Catholic profession or whether they are being drawn away by centrifugal forces whose focal point is the spirit of the world and not that of Christ. In this sense pluralism is a healthy phenomenon. It ceases to be so when it becomes sectarianism. The characteristic of sectarianism is the attribution of absolute truth to only one point of view, which, as point of view related to the entirety of doctrine, is valid, but flies off at a tangent as soon as it becomes exclusive and dissociates itself from the unity of love and faith of the main body of believers. This is the time to intervene. It may be a distasteful task, but it is required by charity towards the weaker brethren whose spirit is not strong enough to discern for themselves.

The magisterium today is becoming more and more aware of its social role. This does not mean that the Church should intervene in the functions of the state, but it should ceaselessly remind the faithful that through their love of Christ, especially of the suffering Christ, they should become the leaven which transforms society. It is easier to condemn errors within the Church than to speak out fearlessly against oppression and injustice in society at large, especially, as happens often especially behind the Iron Curtain, when a pastor has to suffer for it. This is the prophetic function of the Church which the Council has underlined so clearly.

Lastly, in this age of contestation, the bond of love and unity is maintained much more by means of patient dialogue than by the use of force. We all know that authority today is no enviable seat. We would render it easier to administer, however, if we stopped looking on our pastors as ecclesiastical policemen, and considered them more healthily as those who bear a heavy burden for our sakes—that our relationship with Christ may be defended and furthered.

Footnotes

1. Cited according to W. M. Abbott, *The Documents of Vatican II* (New York, 1966) 47-50.

2. *De pudicitia* 1, 6.

3. Eusebius, *Historia ecclesiastica* 5, 16-19. It was long thought that Pope Zephyrinus had condemned this movement in the year 200, but the condemnation once attributed to him should rather be ascribed to Agrippinus, bishop of Carthage; see DS 43.

4. See Irenaeus, *Adversus haereses* 3, 3, 1.

5. DS 101.

6. In the Council of Nicaea, DS 130

7. *Ad Smyrnos* 7, 1.

8. *Adversus haereses* 3, 24, 1.

9. *Ibid.*, 4, 26, 2.

10. *Acta Apostolicae Sedis* 59 (1967) 257-299.

11. *Ibid.*, 63 (1971) 401-441.

CHAPTER THREE

The Magisterium, the Bishops, and the Theologians

Most Reverend David M. Maloney

I have a concise *Theological Dictionary* in an English edition published in 1965 which tells me that the Magisterium is "the Church's active competence, juridically embodied, to prolong by its witness God's self-communicative self-revelation in Christ, which necessarily inheres in the Church (as the eschatologically definitive community of believers in Christ, founded by Him as an hierarchical society, empowered by a mission to bear testimony to Christ), and which demands obedience." [1]

That definition may explain my own conviction that it is indispensable to preface any discussion of the magisterium with those fundamental notions about the Church, its mystery, its nature, its purpose, the qualities with which the Lord endowed it, which make it possible to see the magisterium for what it is. Any discussion which would start out cold by presenting a definition or description without such context would inevitably open itself to misunderstanding and even distortion, and especially to the misunderstanding widely prevalent today which sees the magisterium only in juridical terms and authoritarian connotations. For the Catholic concept of the magisterium and its work is simply a part — a very necessary part, but a part — of the Catholic concept of the Church of Christ and of the work Christ gave the Church to do, in the on-going ministry by which He Himself, with the Holy Spirit, continues to shepherd, to teach, to guide, to direct and to govern His people.

Obviously, it is impossible to give in a short talk any adequate idea of the mystery and the divinely commissioned work of the Church. The very facets of the mystery are bewildering.

We can begin by insisting that the mystery is the mystery of a unity, not simply a group of parallel ways of conceiving of the Church, a variety of paradigms of the Church. I propose *that* as the first necessary concept: namely, there *is* a Catholic doctrine about the Church. It *is* a doctrine which includes mystery in that way so happily and expertly presented by Paul VI in his address of September 29, 1963, opening the second session of the Second Vatican Council and directing the work of the bishops especially to the document setting forth doctrine about the Church. It is a concept which, with all its richness, *remains a unity,* as the Body of Christ which it describes and identifies, remains a unity. The fact of mystery in the very nature of the Church does not preclude clear and authentic Catholic doctrine "de ecclesia"; it is not a doctrine *in fieri,* being worked out today as though *ex nihilo.*[2]

Such a concept of the depth of the mystery of the Church is not new to this century. With all respect to those who love to contrast our wisdom and the richness of our current ecclesiology with what they call the 19th century manuals, we must acknowledge that the ideas we treasure today are to be found in the documents of an earlier day, with a richness that astonishes one who first reads them. They can be found with lengthy exposition in such writers as Billot, Franzelin, Perrone, Scheeben (lest we seem hopelessly "Roman") and in Newman. It is difficult to overemphasize the traditional in

Newman; it is that which gives such value to what was innovative in his thought—he drew on his extensive knowledge of tradition, in which he was well grounded from his Anglican days, and on his contact with the contemporary Roman theologians of his day. The same richness is to be found in the Post-Tridentines like Suarez and Bellarmine; *i fideli, chi sono veramente la chiesa;* not to mention the Medievalists, early and late, and the Fathers.

It is out of such ecclesiology that we should *derive* our understanding of the magisterium, and in the context of such rich ecclesiology that we should *pursue* our understanding of it and of its work.

The present Pontiff, in his first encyclical, *Ecclesiam Suam,*[3] dwelt at some length on this unitive understanding of the Church and of its mystery.

"The mystery of the Church is not a mere object of theological knowledge; it is something to be lived, (something attainable by a sort of supernatural illative process), something that the believer can have a kind of connatural experience of, even before arriving at a clear notion of it. Moreover, the community of the faithful can be profoundly certain of its participation in the Mystical Body of Christ when it realizes that by divine institution, the ministry of the hierarchy of the Church is there, to give it a beginning, to give it birth (cf. Gal. 4:19; 1 Cor. 4:15), to teach and sanctify and direct it. It is by means of this divine instrumentality that Christ communicates to His mystical members the marvels of His truth and of His grace, and confers to His Mystical Body as it travels its pilgrim's way through time its visible structure, its sublime unity, its ability to function organically, its harmonious complexity, its spiritual beauty.

"Images do not suffice to translate into meaningful language the full reality and depth of this mystery.

However, after dwelling on the image of the Mystical Body which was suggested by the Apostle Paul, we should especially call to mind one suggested by Christ Himself—that of the edifice for which He is the architect and the builder, an edifice indeed founded on a man who of himself is weak but who was miraculously transformed by Christ into solid rock, that is, endowed with marvelous and ever-lasting indefectibility: "upon this rock I will build my Church." [4]

It is in such context that the Second Vatican Council's *Dogmatic Constitution on the Church* sets forth the existence and the function of a magisterium of the Church. We will notice that it is the classical, the official magisterium that is the topic here, and that it is committed to the bishops of the Church in union with the sovereign Pontiff. We can begin with the conciliar constitution *Dei Verbum Sensus Fidelium.*

It would be a mistake to refer to that treatment without a brief recognition of the conciliar doctrine about the witness which the whole Church gives to Christ. "... It spreads abroad a living witness to Him, especially by means of a life of faith and charity and by offering to God a sacrifice of praise, the tribute of lips which give praise to His name. The entire body of the faithful, anointed as they are by the Holy One, cannot err in matters of belief. They manifest this special property by means of the whole people's supernatural discernment in matters of faith when 'from the bishops down to the last of the lay faithful' (quoting St. Augustine, *De Praed. Sanct.*) they show universal agreement in matters of faith and morals. This discernment in matters of faith is aroused and sustained by the Spirit of truth. It is exercised under the guidance of the sacred teaching authority, in faithful and respectful obedience to which the people of God accepts what is not just the word of men but the true word of God. By

this means the people of God adheres unwaveringly
to the faith given once and for all to the saints, with
unfailing judgment penetrates more deeply into
its mystery and applies it more fully to its life"
(L.G. 20).

Here we should notice:
1. The whole body of the Church cannot err.
2. The cause of this inerrancy is attributed to
the anointing of the Holy One.
3. It is called a supernatural discernment in
matters of faith.
4. An essential condition is that it is the *whole*
church "from the bishops down to the last of the
lay faithful"—there is no dichotomy between the
hierarchy against the laity, as though the latter alone
were the Church.
5. They show universal agreement; it should not
be necessary to say this does not mean we have a
referendum, and count heads.
6. It is exercised under the guidance of the
sacred teaching authority; again, therefore, socio-
logical surveys attempting to show how many Catholics defy the moral teaching have nothing to do with
the conciliar concept of "sensus fidelium."
7. It speaks of "faithful and respectful obedience"
to the magisterium as something presupposed.
8. The consent given to belief is a consent to
what is not just the word of men, but held to be the
word of God.
Finally, there are two significant results of this
universal consent of the Church to the faith given
to it: one is a *deeper penetration* into the mystery
of the faith (would the Immaculate Conception be
an example?); a second is a *fuller application of the
faith* to life (would this suggest a rich field for application of the lay *actuositas* envisaged by the
council?).

In order to do such witnessing faithfully and effectively, the magisterium has as a first duty to safeguard, to preserve intact, in its totality and its integrity, the message given "once for all to the saints." Only if we remember that, will we understand the constant insistence of Catholic tradition on the Magisterium's duty to "preserve," to "safeguard," — and its repeated reference to the *Depositum Fidei*.

Perhaps one may venture the suggestion that this *"Depositum"* — revelation, as we see it — is the living message which proclaims the gospel of eternal life. It is the unfolding of salvation history as found in both Testaments, with its culmination in the death and resurrection of Jesus, whom it proclaims as Lord and the promised Messiah. It is there, together with all the richness of life already to be found, at least in seed, in the Apostolic Church. It is a Church which continues to live and which has never ceased to declare itself the living Body of Christ, animated by the Holy Spirit and by the charity "diffused in our hearts by the holy spirit who is given to us." Now: *if* it is seen in that way, seen as what I submit it *is*, then those among us today who fear anything static can find rest from their fears. With such a concept of what the *Depositum Fidei* really means, they can feel less threatened by papal and episcopal insistence on this first duty of the Magisterium — to preserve the heritage of faith, the *Depositum*.

The object of magisterial teaching is the full body of a divine revelation, and it can be accepted only on the authority and the dignity of Him from whom it comes. Its acceptance, therefore, will have that quality of divine faith which is something unique, unknown in any other human process of knowledge.

The Magisterium and the Bishops

For purposes of practical approach, I intend now to say something about the part the individual bishop has in the Magisterium. The previous remarks about the magisterium in general would seem to include all that we have time for, here and now, on the work of the college of bishops, the subject of collegiality. All of us know the importance of that aspect of the Magisterium; I think all of us know it would be impossible even to touch on its major aspects in this paper.

It may serve some good, however, to offer some remarks — I hope theologically solid — on the function of the individual bishop as teacher. Here again, to avoid subtle distinctions and endless by-paths, I have in mind the residential bishop.

We should begin by noting that the recent council places the teaching duty of a bishop among the fruits of his sacramental ordination. It also insists that his work as teacher, to a degree which affects the validity and credibility of his teaching, depends on hierarchical union with the college of bishops and with the Roman See. "From the tradition, which is expressed especially in liturgical rites and in the practice of both the Church of the East and of the West, it is clear that, by means of the imposition of hands and the words of consecration, the grace of the Holy Spirit is conferred, and the sacred character impressed, in such a way that bishops in an eminent and visible way sustain the role of Christ Himself as teacher, shepherd and high priest, and that they act in His person" (L.G., art. 21). " ... Hence, a man is constituted a member of the episcopal body in virtue of sacramental consecration and hierarchical communion with the head and members of the body." [5]

Moreover, like the entire magisterial office, the teaching office of the individual bishop, together with his entire ministry, is one of ministry for the service of his people and the building up of the universal Church. He can never be considered, nor consider himself in his exercise of his episcopal office, as separated from the episcopal college, the universal Church, the peculiar bond that ties him to those committed to his personal care, and above all, the union which keeps him in hierarchical communion with the Roman Pontiff. Nor may his work as teacher be thought of out of the context we have already given, the context of the whole Church of Christ in its mystery as sacrament of Christ and mystical Body of the Savior.

In such a context, his work is to teach, to preach the gospel, the truth of Christ. He is, in his own diocese, the voice of the shepherd, having his mandate from Christ. In the words of the Council, "as vicar and ambassador of Christ, he governs the particular church entrusted to him." And the Council lists the way he works: "by counsel, exhortation, example...by authority and sacred power." It is a power he should use only to build up his flock, but he does use it "in Christ's name."[6]

He is, therefore, an authentic teacher, *the* authentic teacher of the faith in his own diocese. That imposes a fearful responsibility. He must speak the doctrine of faith, he must preach it to believer and non-believer. It is his duty to cherish and preserve unsullied and undiminished the entire deposit of faith. He must be its interpreter and defender. It is for him to condemn error, when it appears. It will be his duty, sometimes, to warn those toying with dangerous novelties, to correct misunderstandings of Catholic teaching, to reprove the presumptuous and foolhardy, and with great prudence and only after exhausting all other remedies, it can be his duty to punish those who offend, especially if their offense be in teaching.

The nature of his work is that of a witness to the faith. By himself, he speaks by virtue of an office received from Christ, but by himself, that office does not include infallibility. His words and his actions will be subject to correction by the general teaching and practice of his brother bishops. Before all else, they will be subject to correction by the Holy See. His people can know that he acts and speaks within the limits of his authentic role when they see that he is in harmony, first of all with the Holy Father, and also with the other bishops of the region and of the world. The subject of his teaching must be, by a sacred duty, the faith of the Church, not his own opinions — although he has a reasonable liberty to speak his opinion when he thinks it serves the common good and when he makes it clear that he speaks an opinion, not authentic doctrine.

Like all his brother bishops, singly and collectively, he has that grave duty of being loyal to the teaching given by the Word of God, both oral and written, and he must ever regard himself as the servant of the Deposit of Faith, of tradition, of the Scriptures — in no way the master. He must remain the faithful guardian, devoted to the treasury of the faith which has been placed in his keeping.[7]

In the exercise of his office he will have need of prayer and study. He will depend heavily, and is happy that he is able to find them, on reliable theologians and scholars both in his own diocese and in other parts of the country and the world. He will study to be mindful always that it is his office to minister to others. He will feel humbly his own need to be ministered to by others in the very times that he strives to carry out his own ministry as a faithful steward of God.

And he will need to keep always before him the admonition given him when he was ordained a bishop:

After addressing the community of the Church on the office of a bishop, the ordaining prelate turned to him and said: "You, beloved brother, have been chosen by the Lord — Proclaim the message whether it be welcome or unwelcome; correct error with the greatest patience and in a spirit of teaching. ...As a steward of the mysteries of Christ in the church assigned to you, be a faithful supervisor and guardian. Are you resolved by the grace of the Holy Spirit to discharge to the end of your life the office entrusted to us by the apostles, which is about to be passed on to you by imposition of our hands? Are you resolved to be faithful and constant in proclaiming the gospel of Christ? Are you resolved to maintain the content of faith, entire and uncorrupted, as handed down by the apostles and professed by the Church at all times and places? Are you resolved to be loyal in your obedience to the successor of Saint Peter the apostle?"

It is of such duties to the faith that a bishop thinks when he hears the word "magisterium." Concerning the duties common to all bishops in their ministry of the Word of God to our people, Pope Paul on December 8, 1970, addressed an exhortation to fidelity. He asked us to be mindful of the pledge sent by the bishops at the Council in 1962 in the opening days of their deliberations, promising a common effort to speak to the world the integral and unsullied word of God, hoping that we might put that word in language apt for this time so that men might both understand it and be led to embrace it.

He reminded us that the lasting duty of the episcopal office is to give the people the word of God in all its fullness. The bishop must stand, firm and unmoved, on the ground of tradition and the Sacred Scriptures in order to give the whole people of God food which is the word of God. This they must do without interruption, teaching unceasingly, teaching truth, striving to help it grow

among men. He must give the truth without adultera-
tion, with great charity. For it is given to us by the
imposition of hands to preserve the faith pure and
entire. People have a right to hear the word of God
in its entirety.

The Pope then cited with approval a message
of the German bishops, issued in December of 1968,
that such work can only be done in the Church, in
the community of the Church, and he repeated their
warning against a dangerous misunderstanding of
what the Council had said about freedom of conscience. He pointed out with them that the freedom
of conscience spoken of by the Vatican Council is a
freedom men have, because God will not force them,
to accept or to reject the faith. It is not a freedom
to judge for themselves what is to be the content
of faith; that judgment is the work and the duty of the
bishops, of the magisterium.[8]

The Magisterium and the Theologians

In the series of theses which were proposed by
the International Theological Commission in June,
1976[9] concerning the relationship between the
ecclesiastical magisterium and theology, much
reference was made to an address given by Pope
Paul to a gathering of theologians in Rome — on
October 1, 1976[10] (cf. AAS, p. 889ff., vol. 58). It seems
not inappropriate therefore to turn to that address
for some ideas about the work of the theologian in
the Church and his relations with the teaching office.

The common root from which both the magisterium and the theologians draw their teaching is
divine revelation, a revelation given by the Holy
Spirit to the Catholic Church, and preserved by the
Holy Spirit in that Church.

The Church has been constituted by the Lord a
faithful teacher of His truth, and it enjoys from Him

the charism of indefectibility in the truth He gave for the salvation of the world (shades of H. Küng).

Hence, the Church continues to call Herself the pillar and ground of truth.

For the theologian, the proximate and the universal norm of indefectible truth is to be found only in the authentic magisterium, and this is by the will of Christ. For the theologian's work concerns the truth of faith, the deposit of faith, and the work of faithfully preserving that and infallibly interpreting it belong to the magisterium. In this connection, the Pope recalled that the promise of the Holy Spirit was given to the apostles, as was the power to teach with the authority of Christ.

The magisterium and the theologian pursue the same goal, work for the same purposes.

They strive to safeguard the deposit of sacred revelation;

to explore its meaning more deeply;

to expound it;

to teach it;

to defend it.

Both work to enlighten the Church by exposition of divine truth, and both work for men and their salvation.

The Pope signaled out these differences, concentrating on the theologian.

Theology, using reason illumined by faith, and always docile to the light of the Holy Spirit, engages in the work of exploring and seeking after a more perfect knowledge of the truths of divine revelation.

The theologian offers the results of his labor to the Christian community and especially to the magisterium, so that through the teaching given by the ecclesiastical hierarchy, the whole Christian people may progress, may gain further understanding of the faith and of the depths of its mysteries.

The theologian undertakes his work so that the truth taught by the magisterium may be more widely known, may be illustrated, clarified, fortified. (Here I dare add a personal interpretation of the Pope's meaning: the theologian works so that the validity of the magisterium's teaching and conclusions may be fortified "humaniter" by drawing natural truth to the defense of authentic teaching.)

As examples of what I might call direct service to the Magisterium, I might suggest the appeal made by Pope Paul in *Humanae Vitae*[11] to experts to explore, clarify, enrich the human sources for the argument from natural law in defense of the traditional teaching on contraception. Another, of different kind, would be the invitation made by the Congregation for the Doctrine of the Faith for investigation, contemplation, enrichment of the *rationes convenientiae* given in the last two sections of its declarations about ordination of women; still another would be the field open for historical investigation about the data of tradition bearing on the Church's constant conviction that priestly ordination is reserved to the male sex.[12] The point is: this is not the *only* way theology serves the Church. It is *one* way, and a legitimate field of theological activity.

With further regard to the relations of theological studies and the vigilance of the Magisterium, I venture these thoughts.

We do not need instant scientific proof that the Church is right every time someone questions the cogency of a traditional argument in favor of accepted Catholic teaching. The doctrines of the faith do not take their validity from the scientific theological proofs, as they are often called, offered by theologians or biblicists. Their validity rests upon the witness given by the Catholic Church that a particular dogma is a part of the integral faith; that witness is given by sacred tradition, by the biblical texts correctly read in the community of the Church under the guidance of the magisterium. And I put it to you that this will usually be by no means what is currently ridiculed as the "proof-text" approach. The magisterium, as interpreter, authorized interpreter and judge of tradition and scripture, remains the proximate source of our doctrine.

It is well that our scholars seek to be informed, and to be able to answer questions, whether these come from Catholics or non-Catholics. But we should all start out with the assurance of Faith that the Church is still the credible custodian of the truth committed to Her by Christ, and is competent to declare accurately, within the limits of human language, what is to be held as of faith. We need the calm assurance that Christ does keep His promise to be with the teachers of the Church (the Pope and bishops). With great respect we need to recognize that theologians as such are not and do not pretend to be (in such statements as those I have been referring to) a part of that official magisterium. We need calm faith that the teaching Church is in very fact kept from error by the aid of the Holy Spirit as it goes on teaching the full and integral and undistorted revelation Christ gave to the world.

And with such calm faith, I submit we can then be prepared, all of us, bishops and faithful together, to give to the theological community a sincere and respectful confidence, with the kind of freedom it asks for in its 1976 theses, as it pursues its special and valuable work; moreover, we will look on that work as a part of the providential care God gives to the community of faith through the Holy Spirit. It will be a confidence that expects a corresponding sense of responsibility, a sense of responsibility we can expect theologians to evidence in a way commensurate with its own common self-respect and its own shared faith in the common doctrinal heritage of the Church. It will be a confidence always bound by the limits set by the divinely established nature of the Church, in which all members cooperate in cherishing and guarding the faith, motivated by a deep love for the faith, and guided and led by its pastors in union with the successor of Peter. It will be a confidence marked by the love all of us share, all of us in this mysterious, living, grace-filled Body of Christ, a love for the faith that makes us one.

The theologian, precisely as a theologian, is one who begins with the teaching of the Faith. In other words, he is first of all a believer before he is a theologian. It is as a believer that he does his work in the field of theology. He bends his efforts and uses his skills, his abilities, gathering whatever he can gather from the findings of human sciences and philosophy, as well as from the monuments and documents of tradition and the magisterium — all this in order to build up or contribute to a reasoned, scientific statement of the Faith.

He will have in special view the needs and the intellectual frame of the men of his own age.

As a theologian, he looks for answers to give us, the faithful and the magisterium. He asks questions; and he studies questions others are asking. His purpose is to find answers; to analyze the questions; to localize the source of the questions or difficulties that others have voiced; to validate the logic of theological reasons proposed in expounding the Faith; to explore critically, but always as a believer, the scriptural, the traditional, the theological arguments used by the Church community in expounding its Faith.

With or without a canonical mission (as the term is used in the theses of the International Theological Commission), the theologian teaches as a member of the Body of the Church. In this (I hope I say without egregious error), his teaching, and that of the theologians as a group, is distinct from that of the official *ecclesia docens*. He has a place with catechists, with the parish priest, with the faculties of Catholic schools and universities. In a different way, he aids and shares to some qualified extent with the ordinary teaching work of a bishop in his diocese—and with the college of bishops. For all are members of the Church. As the official magisterium is distinct in its own teaching, in that community of the Church, so the theologian has a distinct place of his own—because of the scholastic and scientific competence necessary—in this common collaboration of the whole Church in the teaching work of the Magisterium. It would seem difficult, however, to classify theology as a separate and distinct Magisterium, except in a very broad sense, the sense used by St. Thomas.[13]

The work of the theologian, placed as it is by its nature in relation to the data of the faith and the magisterium, does not mean at all that he will always approach his subject with these data as premises from which his conclusions will be drawn. He will be correctly convinced that he must often prescind by a kind of methodical (fictitious) doubt, in order better to explore, expound, and study the conclusions of empirical data, historical research, objective analysis of a text or document. He will think rightly that the more critical his study is, the more valuable service he renders to the end result of theology—the progress and deepening of our understanding of the faith. In no way does this minimize his commitment to the Faith, or the genuine devotion he has to the Church and its teaching.

As a Catholic community, we have no need to be disturbed by learned discussions of points which do not much affect us in our practical living of the faith. Theologians can discuss whether a given doctrine is to be found in a given scriptural text. They cannot change the doctrine, and (save in very rare instances) they have no wish to do so. Their intention is not to call the doctrine into question, but perhaps to find more solid bases on which it rests. Their purpose is also to enrich the doctrine.

There persists a question, and it is this: is it always possible to discern when a writer is offering acceptable theological views, and when he is in conflict with the Church's doctrine?

It is to answer such questions, when there is serious pastoral need, that the magisterium must intervene, either on the local, the regional, or the universal scale — scil. by action of the Holy See.

The vigilance over faith will most often be, and is usually, exercised by positive teaching of truth, with insistence on the traditional and accepted understanding of the meaning given to dogma and moral precept in the community of the Church, under the leadership especially of the Holy See. It will often be exercised in union with other bishops in such things as collective pastoral letters. Such warnings as are necessary in view of incipient or widespread errors will be incorporated into positive and affirmative statements of the Faith. The diocesan bishop will normally act in the same way.

When it becomes necessary to warn against a particular error, or popularly spread novelty, that will be done; it is usually done after consultation (unless it is an obvious case) and most of the time it will be the error, not the author, that is warned against. This does not rule out cases in which a particular book contains serious error, and needs to be mentioned. Such a case was the book of Hans Küng on Infallibility[14] — which was anything but an inquiry! The Bishops of Italy[15] and Germany[16] and France,[17] acting as separate groups, issued monitums about it. Because of the notoriety, a regional statement was issued by the bishops of one American province. Such things are rare. It will be even much rarer for an individual bishop to warn against a particular book.

Footnotes

1. K. Rahner, H. Vorgrimler, *Theological Dictionary* (London, 1965) 268.
2. *Acta Apostolicae Sedis* 55 (1963) 847-850.
3. *Acta Apostolicae Sedis* 56 (1964) 609-659.
4. *Acta Apostolicae Sedis* 56, 624f.
5. *Lumen Gentium*, paragraph 22.
6. *Lumen Gentium*, paragraph 27.
7. *Lumen Gentium*, paragraphs 23-25.
8. *Acta Apostolicae Sedis* 63 (1971) 97-106.
9. International Theological Commission, *Twelve Theses on the Relationship between the Ecclesiastical Magisterium and Theology* (Washington, 1977).
10. *Acta Apostolicae Sedis* 58 (1966) 889-896.
11. *Acta Apostolicae Sedis* 60 (1968) 498.
12. *Acta Apostolicae Sedis* 69 (1970) 108-116.
13. *IV Sententiarum* d. 19, q. 2.
14. H. Küng, *Infallibility? An Inquiry* (New York, 1971).
15. French translation in *Documentation Catholique* 53 (1971) 246.
16. French translation in *Documentation Catholique* 53, 245; see also later statement, *ibid.* 330.
17. *Documentation Catholique* 53, 336f.

CHAPTER FOUR

The Magisterium and Moral Theology

William E. May

In May, 1968, John Cardinal Heenan said that "today what the Pope says is by no means accepted as authoritative by all Catholic theologians. An article in the periodical *Concilium* is as likely to win their respect as a papal encyclical. The decline in the magisterium is one of the most significant developments in the post-Conciliar Church."[1] Cardinal Heenan's words, it can safely be said, are as applicable today, a decade later, as they were in 1968. In fact, today we are faced, as Karl Rahner has noted, with "the phenomenon of individuals only *partially* identifying themselves with [the Church].... Now in this situation there is a very real danger that under cover of the watchword of democracy many individuals will be carried away from the Church into positions which are un-Christian and un-Catholic."[2]

One factor that has, in my judgment, contributed to this situation is the conflict that frequently arises today between the teachings of the magisterium and the teachings of theologians, in particular, of moral theologians, on questions of critical significance in the daily lives of ordinary people. This conflict naturally gives rise to questions about the meaning of the magisterium, the assent due to its teachings, and the relationship between the teachings of the magisterium and the teachings of the theologians; it has undoubtedly been the cause of considerable puzzlement and confusion in the minds of ordinary Catholics.

Another factor contributing to this situation is the view, expressed by Avery Dulles, S.J., that it is necessary to be somewhat vague in answering the question "who constitute the magisterium?" For Dulles and those who agree with him, the Pope and bishops (the *hierarchical* or *official* magisterium) have an undoubted *jurisdictional* supremacy of authority within the Church[3] and have "general charge of the Church's teaching, as well as its worship and discipline."[4] But for him and others the theologians exercise a type of *doctrinal* magisterium[5] predicated upon a professional competence which the official magisterium apparently lacks.[6] Thus the question arises, which of these magisteria—the official (hierarchical) or the doctrinal—is to be followed when their teachings are opposed?[7]

In what follows I do not intend to deal fully with the complex of issues involved in these questions. I do intend, however, to present some reflections on the meaning of the ecclesial magisterium, the assent due to its teachings, and the relationship of its teachings to the work of the Catholic scholar—in particular, the moral theologian—that will, I hope, deal substantively with some of the basic issues at stake.

The Meaning of the Magisterium[8]

Today the term *magisterium* has a very precise meaning, one given it by the Church in its own understanding of itself as the pillar and ground of truth (cf. 1 Tim. 3:15), against which the gates of hell cannot prevail (Mt. 16:18; Gal. 1:8), and as the community to which Christ Himself entrusted His saving word and work.[9] According to its own understanding of the term, the Church teaches that the magisterium is the authority to teach, in the name of Christ, the truths of the Christian faith and of all that is necessary or useful for the proclamation and defense of these truths.[10] This teaching authority, moreover, is vested in the college of bishops under the headship and leadership of the Roman Pontiff, inasmuch as the bishops are the successors of the apostles and their chief bishop, the Roman Pontiff, the "concrete center of unity and head of the whole episcopate," [11] is the successor of the Apostle Peter, the "Rock" upon whom Christ founded the Church and the one to whom it was said, "Feed my lambs, feed my sheep" (Jn. 15:17) and "strengthen your brothers" (Lk. 22:32).[12] This magisterium, moreover, demands assent by virtue of the authority formally invested in it and not simply by virtue of the contents of the message it teaches.[13] It has authority in teaching over the rest of the faithful in keeping with the constitution of the Church itself.[14]

The magisterium exercises this teaching authority infallibly in a solemn way through an ecumenical council or through a teaching of the Roman Pontiff when, "as the supreme shepherd and teacher of all the faithful he...proclaims by a definitive act some doctrine of faith or morals." [15] The magisterium also exercises its teaching authority infallibly in a more ordinary way when the bishops throughout the world and in unity with the Pope "concur in a single viewpoint as the one which must be held conclusively" on a matter of faith or morals.[16]

The magisterium, moreover, is an authoritative and authentic teacher of Catholic faith and practice even when it exercises its teaching authority in a manner that is not clearly intended to be infallible. When the bishops teach on matters of faith and morals, they "speak in the name of Christ and the faithful are to accept their teaching and adhere to it with a religious assent of soul. This religious submission of will and of mind must be shown in a special way to the authentic teaching authority of the Roman Pontiff, even when he is not speaking *ex cathedra.* That is, it must be shown in such a way that his supreme magisterium is acknowledged with reverence, the judgments made by him are sincerely adhered to, according to his manifest mind and will." [17]

I believe that the foregoing paragraphs accurately summarize the understanding of the magisterium in the precise sense given to that term by the Church itself.[18] As we shall see, special questions center on what has come to be called the "authentic but noninfallible" exercise of the magisterium and the sense in which a "religious assent of soul" is to be given to the teachings of the authentic but noninfallible magisterium. But before taking up these questions and the relationship of the magisterium to the work of Catholic scholars, in particular moral theologians, it is necessary to comment on the meaning of the magisterium as described above.

First of all, it needs to be said that there is a definite need for a magisterium or a teaching authority within the Church. One might almost say that if the magisterium did not exist one would have to invent it. In order to show what I mean here I will offer some reflections inspired by the thought of John Courtney Murray in his book *We Hold These Truths.*[19] Murray's work was a prolonged commentary on the political life of the American people, on the need for a consensus among that people—however pluralistic culturally and otherwise—for it *to be* a people. His reflections, I believe, can be applied analogously to the Church as the people of God.

As Catholic Christians we *do* hold some truths. We hold these truths both because they are a patrimony *and* because they are true. I am not going to try to spell these out, but I think that the point is obvious. There can be and indeed are *arguments* among us about the meaning of these truths (and hence a true pluralism in theologies or in ways of understanding what these truths mean—and more of this later), but these arguments make sense only because they are related to a common consensus. But this consensus, which is a growing reality, has to be articulated and disputes concerning it have to be adjudicated and settled, for if the consensus is not articulated and if the disputes are not adjudicated then there can no longer be a Catholic *people* but only a motley collection of individuals or groups of individuals. Although each of the faithful (including scholars and theologians) has a voice in the articulation of the common, shared consensus, there must ultimately be a center of unity with the authority to express the *mind* of this people, the Church, to distinguish dissenting voices from those that are expressing the shared consensus, and to determine which theologies are compatible with the shared consensus and which are not.[20]

My presupposition, and a presupposition predicated not upon any theological understanding of the magisterium but rooted in the teaching of the Church itself about itself, is that the magisterium as described above *is* this center of unity and the situs of an authoritative power to discern the true from the false in the articulation of the truths we hold as the Catholic people. If the magisterium as described above is *not* this center of unity and situs of authoritative teaching power there would, of necessity, have to be another source to function as the magisterium.

Second, although the precise meaning of *magisterium* as described above is, as Yves Congar has noted, of relatively recent vintage,[21] the *reality* to which it refers is not, as Congar likewise notes.[22] In fact, if we consider that the Church understands itself to be the community of faith in the Lord, then we must, Rahner reminds us, undoubtedly acknowledge "with the ancient Church that the episcopate as a whole possesses an 'infallible' doctrinal authority in all cases where the whole episcopate teaches a doctrine as part of its actual testimony to Christ, to be accepted with an absolute assent of faith (cf. Rouet de Journel, *Enchiridion Patristicum*, 204, 209ff., 242, 296, 298)."[23] The authority of the bishops united with their head, the Pope, to teach on matters of faith and morals is indeed a doctrine that is, in the concrete, "almost identical with the history of the self-understanding of the Church itself, which cannot but understand itself essentially except as the bearer of the gospel message."[24]

Prior to the second third of the nineteenth century it is true that the term *magisterium* was used to designate the teaching of the theologians, and that this term was commonly used to designate their teaching in the Middle Ages. Still the authority behind their teaching consisted *exclusively* in the nature of the arguments and evidence that they advanced to support their positions,[25] and it thus contrasted sharply with the authority of the teaching given by those who had the *magisterium cathedrae pastoralis* as distinguished from the *magisterium cathedrae magistralis*,[26] that is, by those in whom the *reality* of the magisterium as it is understood today was materially located and formally vested.[27] From this it follows that the term *magisterium* today *cannot* be predicated properly of the theologians. To apply this term today, in the precise sense in which it has come to be understood within the Church and in which it is understood by the Church itself in teaching about itself, would be to commit the fallacy of equivocation. There *are not* two magisteria within the Church; there is only one: the magisterium invested in the college of the bishops under the leadership of the Roman Pontiff. To affirm, as do several writers today (e.g., Avery Dulles and Richard McCormick),[28] that there are *two* complementary magisteria within the Church, the "official" or "hierarchical" magisterium of the episcopal college under the Pope and the "doctrinal" magisterium of the theologians,[29] is simply to introduce an unnecessary and intolerable ambiguity into the term and amounts, in my opinion, to a rejection of the Church's own self-understanding of the term. This is not to say that the task of the theologian is to serve the magisterium or to define in any way the task of the theologian—a matter to which I shall return. It is simply to deny that the task of the theologian, or of the corps of theologians, is in any way to be considered as strictly magisterial; it is to reject the legitimacy of predicating the term *magisterium* today of the theologians, simply because that term has taken on a meaning within the life of the Church that precludes its being predicated of others than those in whom the teaching authority of the Church is vested.

Third, some observations are necessary with respect to what has come to be called the authentic noninfallible exercise of the magisterium. It is certainly true that not everything that is taught by the magisterium is infallibly proposed. In this sense it is legitimate to describe such teachings as authentic, authoritative, and *non*infallible. But it would be a serious error to conclude from this that such teachings are fallible, in the sense that they are to be understood as being merely probable opinions or as being at best only presumptively true.[30] It may well be that the teachings in question *are* infallibly true, in the sense that they really are true and that opinions contradicting them are really erroneous.[31] They simply are not being infallibly proposed by the magisterium. Obviously the truths of Christ's divinity, of His real presence in the Eucharist, of the sacramentality of marriage, of the Pope's primacy and infallibility, of the Virgin's immaculate conception and assumption were *infallibly true* prior to their being infallibly taught by the ecclesial magisterium. Above all, it would be a serious demeaning of the "authentic, noninfallible teachings of the magisterium" to regard

them as simply "official" points of view to be publicly presented but privately questioned.[32]

Fourth, it is necessary to offer some observations
about the magisterium and moral matters in particular. Some writers, for instance Daniel Maguire[33]
and Charles E. Curran,[34] have asserted that nothing
in the field of morals has been taught infallibly by
the Church through the ecclesial magisterium. To
me it seems that these authors have erroneously
limited infallible teachings to teachings that are
articulated solemnly in ecumenical councils or
through papal *ex cathedra* pronouncements. Although
this is not the place to develop this subject, I believe
that a very good case can be made to show that many
of the moral teachings of the Church dealing with
concrete, specifiable kinds of moral activity are
infallibly taught (and, it can be added, infallibly
believed by the faithful). Here I am thinking specifically of the morality that is set forth in the Commandments as these have been understood throughout
the history of the Church, a history that has indeed
seen a development in the understanding of the
Commandments but one in which there has been a
continuity in that development. Never, for example,
in the history of the Church has the ecclesial magisterium suggested that the deliberate destruction of
innocent human life might be morally justifiable;
rather it has never failed to insist that innocent human
life may never be directly attacked.[35] Never, in the
history of the Church, has the magisterium hinted
that sexual coition outside the covenant of marriage
can be morally good; on the contrary, the magisterium has consistently taught (and with it, I might add,
the theologians,[36] at least until the days of Michael
Valente[37] and the Catholic Theological Society of
America report on human sexuality[38]) that adultery,
fornication, and other modes of nonmarital sexual
union are seriously wrong and incompatible with
the life of the Christian who has put on Christ and

become one body with Him. I do not intend to pursue this very important subject further here, but there is surely reason to hold that some quite specific moral teachings of the magisterium are in fact taught infallibly by the ordinary exercise of that magisterium and are held by the faithful as part of the *sensus fidelium*.[39] The assertion that *no* teachings of the magisterium on moral issues are infallibly proposed is simply that: an assertion.

Finally, it is important to note that the teachings of the magisterium are precisely that—teachings.[40] They are not to be regarded as imperial edicts of an authoritarian body anxious to preserve its status— something that is, unfortunately, implied by Avery Dulles.[41] Rather they are to be considered as the intelligent, reflective expression of the *mind* of the Church on matters pertaining to the faith and life of the Catholic people. They are thus proposed as *truths* that the faithful are to make their own through intelligent acts.

The Question of the "Religious Assent of Soul"

With these observations on the meaning of magisterium in mind, let us now look, first, at the question of the "religious assent of soul" that is to be given to the teachings of the authentic yet non-infallible magisterium and, second, to the more general topic of the relationship between the magisterium and the work of the Catholic scholar, in particular of the moral theologian.

Here it must first be said that the magisterium itself respects the integrity and personal responsibility that characterize the people of God (in fact, all people everywhere) as conscientious, free persons whose minds and hearts can be coerced by no external power and who must answer for their lives before God, who summons them to an ever-deeper grasp of truth.[42] Since this is so, it would seem to be erroneous to suppose that the magisterium, in exercising its teaching office, expects blind, unthinking obedience to its teachings. The "religious assent of soul" of which Vatican II speaks must not be understood as demanding this kind of servile assent; nor, I must add, need the teaching of Vatican II on this question be dismissed, as it is being dismissed by some today (e.g., McCormick), as simply a reflection of an outmoded ecclesiology.[43] Rather it would appear that, in speaking of this "religious assent of soul" the Council is to be understood as summoning the faithful to assent internally and externally to its teachings, including those authentically yet noninfallibly proposed, precisely because of its conviction that those teachings are true *and* precisely because those teachings are proposed as true by the Church itself in the exercise of the *teaching authority* given it by Christ Himself and vested within the magisterium. To put it another way, in exercising its authority to teach the magisterium is appealing to the faithful as persons of *faith* and as persons with a *conscience*. The magisterium appeals to the faith of the faithful with the expectation that the faithful will, in faith, make their own through acts of faithful understanding the teachings of the magisterium. It appeals to the conscience of the faithful, with the recognition that there can at times be a conflict within the conscience of the faithful with respect to a specific teaching,[44] and that this conflict can only be resolved within the depths of the faithful themselves as they seek conscientiously and in faith to answer the summons of God Himself to the truth, a summons inwardly given them by God and one corroborated by the magisterium in the exercise of its teaching authority.[45]

This, I believe, is what is at the heart of the magisterium's summons to the faithful to accept its teachings with a "religious assent of soul." Those teachings are not simply "offered to the faithful," as McCormick once suggested.[46] They are expressed *precisely with a summons to cleave to them in faith*. Perhaps this is what McCormick himself was suggesting when he referred to "a connatural eagerness" on the part of the faithful to assent to the teachings of the magisterium. There is, I believe, in the faithful an eagerness to give this assent, an eagerness rooted in the faith of the faithful, in their belief that the magisterium would not teach something pertaining to their lives as believing and practicing Catholics unless the magisterium were itself convinced that the teaching in question was true and intrinsically related to the gospel of salvation or to something necessarily connected with this saving gospel.

In other words, the teachings of the authentic, noninfallible magisterium do bind the consciences of the faithful to assent, in faith, to these teachings; *but they bind the conscience in the way that conscience is bound,* namely with respect for the absolute inviolability of personal conscience.[47] Thus dissent from such teachings must be recognized as a possibility that at times, from the perspective of the believing subject, can be realized; for the believing subject must, in the inner sanctuary of his conscience where he is alone with God,[48] make his own personal judgments about the meaning of his life and his choices.

Nonetheless, there can never be a "double truth," one a truth for the magisterium's teachings and another a truth for personal conscience. Because of the faithful Catholic's *faith* that Jesus has not left us orphans but has indeed commissioned the episcopate under the headship of the Roman Pontiff to teach in His name, one not only presumes but anticipates that the truth lies with the teachings of the magisterium. To conclude that this teaching is erroneous is to reach a judgment that a faithful

Catholic ought reach only with the most extreme reluctance; were one to reach this judgment frequently and, as it were, almost spontaneously, this would (it seems to me) be a very serious matter. It ought to cause such a person to stop short and begin to reflect quite critically upon his own processes of judging. McCormick expressed the matter here under consideration quite perceptively, in my opinion, almost a decade ago. Then, in speaking of the "connatural eagerness" that ought to characterize the response of the faithful to the teachings of the magisterium, McCormick noted that this eagerness should be concretized in several specific ways, and among these would be "a readiness to reassess one's own positions in light of this teaching, an attempt to see if this teaching can be supported on grounds other than those proposed, and a humble realization of the limitations imposed by one's own background."[49]

If such specific ways of concretizing the prompting of faith to assent interiorly to the teachings of the magisterium were seriously undertaken, there would, in my opinion, be a lessening of the tendency observable today to question almost immediately the teachings of the magisterium and to conclude that these teachings are fallible (in the sense of erroneous) because they are predicated upon an outdated, physicalistic, static understanding of the human person and his acts.[50]

The Relationship of the Magisterium to the Scholar, in Particular, to the Moral Theologian

How is the magisterium related to the scholarly community, in particular, the theological community? According to Dulles,[51] McCormick,[52] and other contemporary observers,[53] the Neoscholastic theology regnant in the nineteenth and early twentieth

centuries saw the scholarly community, in particular
the theologians, in the service of the magisterium.
They believe that this is an inadequate way of expressing this relationship, for they believe that in
effect it *separates* the magisterium from the Church
and that it is a serious demeaning of the work of
theologians.[54] With Yves Congar[55] they propose that
both the magisterium and the scholar (in particular
the theologians who, for Dulles and McCormick,
constitute the "*doctrinal* magisterium") are in the
service of the truth. They thus suggest that there
are in fact two complementary magisteria within
the Church, the official hierarchical magisteriun. of
the bishops under the Pope, concerned with the
"good order" of the community, and the scientific
or doctrinal magisterium of the theologians.[56]

With these writers I agree that the relationship
between the magisterium and the scholarly community, in particular the theological community,
is *not* one in which scholars and theologians have
as their task the "serving" of the magisterium *in the*
sense of a servile "yea-saying" and, as it were, a
"rubber-stamping" of the teachings of the magis-
terium. To consider the relationship in this way
would be a serious disparagement of the role of the
scholar and of the scholar-theologian. There. is
surely a sense in which both the magisterium and
the scholar (including the theologian) are in a common service to the truth, and there is a sense in
which the magisterium and the scholar "complement"
one another.

Yet it is necessary to take issue with Dulles and
McCormick and others who speak of a twofold magisterium within the Church. There is surely no question
of any equality between the magisterium and the
scholarly, theological community. The complementarity that exists between them is not analogous
to the complementarity of male and female, two
differing yet complementary expressions of epiph-

anies of the living God. For the magisterium, as the magisterium itself understands itself in expressing the mind of the *whole Church,* clearly understands itself as divine and uniquely commissioned to articulate the truths of faith and of Catholic life and to have the power to determine whether particular theological and other scholarly formulations are, in truth, compatible or not with the Church's own understanding of itself and of the truths committed to it. *There are not,* as noted earlier, *two complementary magisteria within the Church,* one the "official" magisterium of the episcopal college under the leadership of the Pope and the other the "scientific" or "doctrinal" magisterium of the corps of theologians. There is only *one* magisterium,[57] and the Catholic scholar, in articulating his/her positions, his/her expressions of the truth, is to recognize this and is to be willing to let his/her positions be judged by the magisterium and to be willing to accept these judgments. An unwillingness to do so is indicative of a desire to usurp for oneself the *teaching* office divinely vested in the magisterium.

This leads to some comments on "pluralism" in theology. There is indeed, and rightly so, a plurality of theologies within the Church—different ways of understanding the truths of faith. These theologies, moreover, are not only complementary but are also, on many points, contradictory.[58] This is only natural, for the truths of the Catholic faith are so inexhaustibly rich in meaning that they can never be fully exhausted and different attempts to understand them (and this is precisely what the theologian is seeking to do) will arise and will, on many points, be incompatible with each other and contradictory to each other. Still it must be remembered that there is always the possibility that theologians will develop positions that are not only incompatible with and contradictory to the positions of other theologians but also incompatible with and

contradictory to the faith itself and all that is necessarily connected with the faith. A particular theology, in other words, can be irreconcilable with
the Church's own understanding of itself.[59] It is indeed one of the functions of the magisterium — and
an indispensable one if the people of God are to be
a people with a common consensus (something that
Dulles clearly recognizes, incidentally[60]) — to be
able to distinguish between positions that are compatible with this understanding and those that
are not.

There is definitely a need for dialogue between
the magisterium and the scholarly community, and
this dialogue should be bilateral. Steps must be
taken to ensure that the "appropriate means" mentioned by the Fathers of Vatican Council II for
ensuring that the voices of all the faithful, including
the theologians, are heard by those who exercise
the ecclesial magisterium.[61] In my judgment there
have been some notable efforts in this direction in
recent years.[62]

The subjects of the magisterium in its precise
sense must live in communion with the Christian
people and the scholarly community, something
that is explicitly recognized in the teachings of the
magisterium itself. But precisely because the magisterium must exist in living communion with the
faithful, whose "*sensus*" is in no way to be equated
with "public opinion,"[63] there come times when
this deep communion needs to be expressed by a
firm *no* on the part of the magisterium. Here I believe
that some remarks of Jacques Maritain concerning
those in authority within a political community can
be applied analogously to those who exist in a state
of true teaching authority within the ecclesial community. Maritain wrote:

> I just said that the representatives of the people
> must be ready to incur the displeasure of the people, if
> their conscience demands it. Now I am saying that they

must carry out their obligations in communion with the people. Are these two statements contradictory? They are not, on the condition that this expression "in communion with the people" be correctly understood. In what can be called the common psyche of the people there is a huge variety of levels and degrees. At the most superficial level there are the momentary trends of opinion, as transient as the waves on the sea, and subjected to all winds of anxiety, fear, particular passions, and particular interests. At the deeper levels, there are the real needs of the multitude. At the deepest level, there is the will to live together, and the obscure consciousness of a common destiny and vocation, and finally the natural trend of the human will, considered in its essence, to the good. Furthermore...people are ordinarily distracted from their most capital aspirations and interests, as a people, by each one's everyday business and suffering. Under such circumstances, to rule in communion with the people means on the one hand educating and awakening the people in the very process of governing them, so as to demand of them, at each progressive step, what they themselves have been made aware of and eager for (I am thinking of a real work of education, grounded on respect for them and trust in them, and in which they are the principal agent...). It means, on the other hand, being intent on what is deep and lasting, and most really worthy of man, in the aspirations and psyche of the people. Thus it is that in incurring the disfavor of the people a ruler can still act in communion with the people, in the truest sense of this expression. And if he is a great ruler, he will perhaps make that endeavor into a renewed and more profound trust.[64]

These words have much to tell us, I believe, about the magisterium of the Church and its relationship to the work of the scholar, in particular of the moral theologian. I believe that the teachings of the magisterium are an endeavor to remind us who we are and what we are to do if we are to be the kind of beings that we are meant to be in Christ. I submit that the scholar/theologian in his/her search for the truth can best find the clues to it by seeking to accept, with connatural eagerness, the teachings of the magisterium.

Since this is the tenth anniversary year of *Humanae Vitae*, I think that it is fitting, in closing, to offer some comments about the authentic teaching of the Church articulated in that expression of the magisterium. Surely the teaching of Paul VI evoked considerable criticism, even contempt, from some theologians. The evidence, however, as such authors as Norbert Rigali[65] and James Schall[66] have noted, shows that in speaking the mind of the Church on the question of human life and its transmission, Pope Paul seriously took into consideration the views of theologians and the sensitivities of the faithful. In addition, it seems to me and to many other observers that the teaching of Pope Paul on this subject is indeed true and capable of being supported by many arguments[67] and that the events of the past decade have in many ways corroborated the truth he was setting forth.[68] It is time, I believe, for theologians to listen seriously and attentively to the teachings of the magisterium and to seek to make these teachings their own. I believe that the path charted by the authors of *Human Sexuality: New Directions in American Catholic Thought*, a path that sees adultery, mate swapping, fully deliberate masturbation, and deeds of a similar kind as possibly "creative and integrative" and compatible with the life of one who has become through baptism one with Christ,[69] will be the result unless this effort by the theologians is made. And this path, I submit, is not one that will enable Catholic Christians to be the beings they are meant to be, living and loving words of the God whose Uncreated Word became one with us and for us in order to give us His life and love.

Footnotes

1. John Cardinal Heenan, "The Authority of the Church," *The Tablet*, 222 (London, May 18, 1968) 488.

2. K. Rahner, "The Teaching Office of the Church in the Present-Day Crisis of Authority," *Theological Investigations*, Vol. 12, trans. by David Bourke (London, 1974), 21.

3. A. Dulles, S.J., *The Survival of Dogma* (New York, 1973), 102, where he explicitly recognizes the "jurisdictional" supremacy of the bishops. On pp. 102 and 103 he distinguishes between the "authentic" magisterium of the bishops and the "doctrinal" magisterium of the theologians. Dulles rightly calls the "primary authority" within the Church Christ and His Spirit (p. 83). But he lumps the hierarchical magisterium of the bishops with the magisterium of the scholars in the category of "secondary authorities" (84-85). While it is true that the authority of Christ and His Spirit is *primary*, it seems to me that the Church itself teaches that the magisterium of the episcopal college under the Pope is an inward participation in this authority of Christ Himself.

4. *Ibid.*, p. 108. In *Survival of Dogma* and in his presidential address to the Catholic Theological Society of America in 1976, "The Theologian and the Magisterium," *Catholic Theological Society of America: Proceedings of the Thirty-First Annual Convention* 31 (1976) 235-246, Dulles *seems* to see the role of the ecclesial or hierarchical magisterium as being concerned with the "good order" of the Church and not so much with doctrinal questions.

5. Dulles, *Survival of Dogma*, 96 and 102, speaks of the doctrinal magisterium of the scholars.

6. *Ibid.*, 97, where Dulles stresses that bishops are "not commonly noted for outstanding capacity in doctrinal matters," and p. 98, where he asks whether "the alleged charisms of the episcopal office... can in fact compensate for the apparent lack of professional competence." It is certainly true that some bishops, perhaps many, are not *professional* theologians and lack the competence one would expect of theologians. But does this mean that they have a doctrinal incompetence? Dulles does not explicitly treat this issue.

7. Dulles does not explicitly treat this issue. Yet the position articulated by R.A. McCormick in his essay, "Personal Conscience," n. 13, in *An American Catechism* (New York: Seabury, 1975), is today quite common. According to this position, when the teachings of the magisterium are contradicted by the teachings of theologians, the faithful may, in forming their consciences, regard the positions of the theologians as "inherently probable or tenable." This means that the teachings of the magisterium on such questions are themselves simply probable and thus need not be followed.

8. Here I think it is necessary to distinguish between a *theology* of the magisterium, which properly belongs to ecclesiology, and the *teaching* of the Church itself on the magisterium. I think that it is essential to make this distinction, and that this distinction is not sufficiently realized by some authors today (e.g., Dulles and McCormick). For brief, quite accurate presentations of the teaching of the Church itself on the magisterium see the articles on "magisterium" by K. Rahner in K. Rahner, (ed.) *Sacramentum Mundi* (New York, 1968) Vol. 3, 351-355 and by L. Bouyer, *Dictionary of Theology* (New York, 1968) 288-290.

9. On this see *Lumen Gentium*, paragraphs 18-20.

10. On this see *Dei Verbum*, paragraph 8.

11. Rahner, "Magisterium," *op. cit.*, 352.

12. *Lumen Gentium*, paragraph 22. Cf. Vatican Council I, Constitution *Pastor aeternus*, chapter 4; DS 3065-3074.

13. On this see Vatican Council I, Constitution *Dei Filius*, chapter 4; DS 3020.

14. *Lumen Gentium*, paragraphs 23-24.

15. *Ibid.*, paragraph 25.

16. *Ibid.* Cf. Vatican Council I, *Dei Filius*, chapter 3; DS 3011.

17. *Lumen Gentium*, paragraph 25.

18. It is important to remember, as Rahner so clearly brings out in his "The Teaching Office of the Church in the Present-Day Crisis of Authority," (*loc. cit.* in note 2), that the magisterium is not to be conceived of as separate from the Church itself, but rather is to be regarded as being in communion with the Church as a whole, as an expression of the entire Church.

19. J.C. Murray, *We Hold These Truths: Catholic Reflections on the American Proposition* (New York, 1960), in particular 27-96.

20. Here it is significant to note that Dulles himself recognizes this need. See *Survival of Dogma*, 100, where he sees that the Church needs an authority in order to express its creed and to speak out in rejecting positions that are incompatible with the creed of Christians.

21. Y. Congar, "Pour une histoire semantique du term 'magisterium,'" *Revue des Sciences Philosophiques et Theologiques* 60 (1976) 85-98, at 94-96.

22. Congar, "Brèf historique des formes du 'magistère' et de ses rélations avec les docteurs," *Revue des Sciences Philosophiques et Theologiques* 60 (1976) 99-112, at p. 103: "Le mot 'magesterium' ne designe pas alors ce que nous appelons 'le Magistère.' Chez les Pères, au moyen age, et jusqu'aux années 20-30 du XIXe s., *magisterium* signifie simplement la situation, la fonction ou l'activité de quelqu'un qui est en position de *magister*, c'est-a-dire d'autorite en un domaine determine.... *L'activite pouvait etre celle d'enseignement*. Dans ce cas, *magisterium rejoignait matériellement le sens moderne de 'magistère'*; mais jamais avant les xixe s., il ne signifie exactement ce que nous appelons 'le Magistère' " (emphasis added).

23. Rahner, "Magisterium," *loc. cit.*, 351.

24. *Ibid.*

25. On this see M.D. Chenu, "'Authentica' et 'magistralia.' Deux lieux theologiques aux XII-XIII siecles," *Divus Thomas* (Piacenza) 28 (1925) 257-285.

26. The terms *"magisterium cathedrae magistralis"* and *"magisterium cathedrae pastoralis"* were used, for example, by Thomas Aquinas in his *In IV Sent.* d. 19, q. 2, a. 2, qua. 2, ad 4. I think it is important to note, with T.C. O'Brien, that "St. Thomas is a forthright papalist. He describes the Pope as the 'vicar of Christ' (2a2ae.39, 1), the 'visible head of the Church' (3a.8, 7,), 'who has the care of the whole Church' (2a2ae.89, 9 ad 3, see *Quodl.* IV, 13)" (in O'Brien's editorial note b on p. 55 of *St. Thomas Aquinas, Summa Theologiae* Vol. 31, *Faith* (2a2ae. 1-17) (New York, 1974). It is also in my opinion important to recall that St. Thomas held that "we must abide rather by the Pope's judgment than by the opinion of any of the theologians, however well versed he may be in divine Scriptures" (*Quodlibetum*

IX , q. 8, corp., in *Quaestiones Quodlibetales,* ed. by R. Spiazzi (Rome: Marietti, 1949), 94.

27. On the *reality* of the magisterium as exercised in the past by bishops and Pope it seems sufficient here to cite simply the testimony of St. Ignatius of Antioch in a letter written circa 106 A.D. and that of Pope St. Leo the Great. Ignatius praises the church at Philadelphia in Asia Minor as "a source of everlasting joy, especially when the members are at one with the bishop and his assistants, the presbyters and deacons, that have been appointed in accordance with the wish of Jesus Christ, and whom He has, by His own will, through the operation of His Holy Spirit, confirmed in loyalty" (*Epistula ad Philadelphienses,* proem.; Migne, *PG:* 5:699). Leo testified that "What Christ, the Lord, the Prince of the Shepherds and Great Shepherd of the Sheep, established in the person of the blessed apostle Peter for the perpetual welfare and everlasting good of the Church must, by the will of the Same, endure without interruption in the Church which, founded on the Rock, will stand firm to the end of the world. Indeed 'no one doubts, in fact it is known to all ages, that the holy and most blessed Peter, prince and head of the apostles, the pillar of faith and foundation of the Catholic Church, received the keys of the kingdom from our Lord Jesus Christ, the Savior and Redeemer of the human race, and even to this time and forever he lives and governs and exercises judgment in his successors' [an internal citation from Philip, papal legate to the Council of Ephesus (431)], the bishops of the Holy Roman See, which was founded by him and consecrated by his blood. Therefore, whoever succeeds Peter in this Chair holds Peter's primacy over the whole Church according to the plan of Christ Himself. Therefore, the disposition made by Truth endures, and blessed Peter, persevering in the rocklike strength he received, has not given up the government of the Church undertaken by him" (*Sermo 3 de Natali Ipsius,* 3; Migne, *PL* 54.146B).

28. For Dulles, see his *Survival of Dogma,* pp. 98-108 and his "The Theologian and the Magisterium," *loc. cit.* (note 4). For McCormick see his "Notes on Moral Theology, *Theological Studies* 38 (1976) 84-100.

29. It seems to me that Dulles believes that the community of theologians has the *teaching* magisterium or *doctrinal* magisterium within the Church, whereas the bishops under the Pope have a *jurisdictional* type of magisterium. Thus he writes (in "The Theologian and the Magisterium") that the bishop "does not so much teach as decide whose teachings may be safely followed. The authority of the approved school of theologians is reinforced by the myth that the bishop is himself the organ of truth" (239). Again, "The *magistri* (i.e., the theologians) teachers by training and by profession have a scientific magisterium, but they are subject to the pastors in what pertains to the good order of the Church as a community of faith and witness" (243). Again, he seems to hold that the job of the bishops is to preach, for the good of the community, what the theologians teach, for he writes: "Magisterial statements (of the pastoral office) should ordinarily express what is already widely accepted in the

Church, *at least by those who have studied the matter in question*" (244). By those "who have studied the matter in question" he obviously means the *magistri* who are theologians. McCormick *(art. cit.)* expresses agreement with Dulles.

30. "Presumptive" truth to teachings of the authentic, noninfallible magisterium seems to be the most that some would attribute. For instance, see McCormick, "Notes on Moral Theology," *Theological Studies* 29 (1968) 715.

31. It is crucially significant to note that the term "noninfallible" is used to designate the authentic teachings of the magisterium that are not proposed infallibly, and not the term "fallible." "Noninfallible" does not mean the same as "fallible," and it is quite erroneous to hold that these teachings of the magisterium are fallible.

32. It is not possible to document this view with any explicit citation. Yet that this is an attitude that is not uncommon in the Church today cannot be denied, and I submit that the readers of *The National Catholic Reporter* would be able to verify this as the attitude expressed in that journal. I, for one, am such a reader.

33. D. Maguire, "Morality and the Magisterium," *Cross Currents* 18 (Winter, 1968), 41-65.

34. C. E. Curran and R. E. Hunt, *Dissent in and for the Church* (New York: Sheed and Ward, 1969), p. 63.

35. On this see J. T. Noonan, "An Almost Absolute Value in History," in J. T. Noonan, ed., *The Morality of Abortion* (Cambridge: Harvard University Press,1970). See also the texts assembled in *Yes to Life*, edited by the Daughters of St. Paul (Boston: Daughters of St. Paul, 1976).

36. In a series of articles to appear in *Theological Studies* 39 (1978) and *The Thomist* 42 (1978) concerned with the notion of intrinsically evil acts, J. Dedek clearly shows that the theologians of the Middle Ages clearly held that no human person, on his own authority, could rightfully destroy innocent human life of deliberate intent or engage in such acts as adultery. The medievals were troubled by Abraham's sacrifice of Isaac, the polygamy of the Fathers, Hosea's wooing of a fornicating woman, etc., but they attributed the liceity of these acts to a divine "dispensation" from the commandments.

37. M. Valente, *Sex: The Radical View of a Catholic Theologian* (New York: Bruce, 1970).

38. A. Kosnik et al..*Human Sexuality: New Directions in American Catholic Thought* (Paramus, N.J.: Paulist Press, 1977).

39. On this question see the article by J. C. Ford and Germain Grisez, "Is the Teaching of the Church on Contraception Infallible?" *Theological Studies* 39 (1978), in press.

40. On this see D. Composti, "Il magisterio ecclesiastico informa o insegna la morale?" *Divinitas* 20 (1976) 199-203.

41. On this see Dulles, "The Theologian and the Magisterium," *loc. cit.*, 241, where he writes: "It has become evident that those in positions of ecclesiastical power are naturally predisposed to accept ideas favorable to their own *class interests. Popes and bishops, there-fore, are inclined to speak in a way that enhances the authority of*

their office" (emphasis added). I believe that Dulles, in making this statement, is unduly influenced by the views of the Tübingen school of sociology.

42. On this see Vatican Council II, *Dignitatis Humanae,* paragraph 2.

43. McCormick and Dulles, and others, seem to believe that paragraph 25 of *Lumen Gentium,* where reference is made the the "religious assent of soul," is simply a reflection of an outmoded ecclesiology. For this see McCormick, "Notes on Moral Theology," *Theological Studies* 29 (1968) 714 and compare what he has to say there with his "Notes on Moral Theology," *Theological Studies* 38 (1977), 99, where he affirms that it has been "quietly accepted" that this passage is dependent on an outdated ecclesiology. See Dulles, "The Theologian and the Magisterium," *loc. cit.,* 240: "Vatican II did not directly challenge the reigning theology of the day. Indeed, article 25 of *Lumen Gentium...* may be interpreted as supporting this theory." Dulles' point is that this article may *now* be regarded as simply reflecting that "reigning theology," one supplanted by more up-to-date ecclesiologies. I think that here it is again necessary to distinguish between a theological understanding of the magisterium and the *teaching* of the Church on the magisterium.

44. Vatican Council II, *Dignitatis Humanae,* paragraph 3.

45. See, on this, Vatican Council II, *Gaudium et Spes,* paragraph 16, where reference is made to the fact that conscience is the inner sanctuary of a person, where one is alone with God, and relate this passage to paragraphs 2 and 3 of *Dignitatis Humanae.*

46. McCormick, "Notes...," *Theological Studies* 29 (1968) 715. Here McCormick states that the "noninfallible Church teachings would be seen as *offered* to the faithful" (emphasis added). He goes on to speak of a "connatural eagerness" to accept these teachings, and in speaking in this way he is, I believe, proceeding in the right direction.

47. Here I think it is helpful to consult Eric D'Arcy, *Conscience and Its Right to Freedom* (New York: Sheed and Ward, 1965) and to relate his work to the understanding of conscience set forth in *Dignitatis Humanae.*

48. See *Gaudium et Spes,* paragraph 16.

49. McCormick, "Notes of Moral Theology," *Theological Studies* 28 (1968) 716.

50. This seems to be the stock, pat objection given by the dissenting theologians to recent statements of the magisterium. It was the standard objection given to the position taken by Paul VI in *Humanae Vitae* (on this cf. the essays by Curran, Häring, and Maguire in C. Curran, ed., *Contraception: Authority and Dissent* (New York: Sheed and Ward, 1969). It is also the standard objection given to the recent "Declaration on Certain Questions Concerning Sexual Ethics," as witnessed by Curran's "Declaration on Sexual Ethics: Summary and Critique," *Linacre Quarterly* 47 (1976) 147-164.

51. Dulles, *Survival of Dogma,* pp. 98-108 and "The Theologian and the Magisterium," *loc. cit.*

52. McCormick, "Notes on Moral Theology," *Theological Studies* 38, (1977), 84-100. See also his "Conscience, Theologians and the Magisterium," *The New Catholic World* 220 (1977) 268-271.

53. C. Curran, *Dissent in and for the Church.*

54. Dulles brings this out particularly well in his *Survival of Dogma.* I am fully in accord with his view that the magisterium must not become separated from the Church as a whole and that, for the magisterium to function properly, it needs to exist in a state of communion and dialogue with the theologians.

55. Congar, "Brèf historique des formes du 'magistère' et de ses rélations avec les docteurs," *loc. cit.* 99-112, at 112.

56. For this, see the texts cited previously, notes 4, 6, and 41.

57. I think that this is demanded by the *unity* of the Church.

58. T. Dubay, "The State of Moral Theology," *Theological Studies* 35 (1974) 482-506, distinguishes between "complementary" and "contradictory" pluralism in theology. Although I have sympathy with this way of speaking, I think that there can be a genuine *contradiction* between theologies that are compatible with Christian faith.

59. On this see the Sacred Congregation for Catholic Education, *The Theological Formation of Future Priests,* (Washington, 1970) paragraphs 65-66.

60. Dulles, *Survival of Dogma,* p. 100.

61. See *Lumen Gentium,* paragraph 25.

62. Here I am thinking particularly of the procedures followed by the bishops of this country in the development of the 1976 pastoral letter on the moral life, *To Live in Christ Jesus.* The committee responsible for preparing this document sent letters to almost 8000 members of various Catholic scholarly societies, inviting them to offer recommendations. They followed this up by submitting drafts of the document to the scholars who had responded, asking them for criticisms and suggestions. Obviously the bishops could not accept all criticisms and suggestions, but they definitely listened to the scholars and sought to understand what they were saying.

63. Dulles, in *Survival of Dogma,* pp. 85-86, seems to me to be equating the "horizontal" channel of authority mediated by public opinion with the *sensus fidelium.* Thus he writes, for example, as follows: "In some Churches, such as the Roman Catholic, the vertical authority of office seems to be yielding somewhat to the horizontal authority of consensus. In nearly all churches, including the Roman Catholic, the continuing authority of long-standing tradition is being challenged by the contemporary authority of public opinion." Here it is instructive to contrast Dulles with Newman and his understanding of the *consensus fidelium.*

64. Jacques Maritain, *Man and the State* (Chicago, 1951), 136-138.

65. Norbert Rigali, S.J., "The Historical Meaning of the *Humanae Vitae* Controversy," *Chicago Studies* 15 (Summer, 1976), pp. 127-139.

66. James V. Schall, S.J., *The Sixth Paul* (New York, 1977), 79-102, where Schall marshalls several arguments to show how deeply Pope Paul listened to the voices of people everywhere and how sub-

sequent events have enabled the prophet-like character of his witness in *Humanae Vitae* to become more and more evident.

67. For some works that, in my judgment, do much to advance strong arguments against contraception, see John Kippley, *Birth Control and the Marriage Covenant* (Collegeville, Minn. 1976); Mary Rosera Joyce, *The Meaning of Contraception* (Collegeville, Minn. 1970); and *Love Responds to Life* (Kenosha, Wis. 1971); James O'Reilly, *The Moral Problem of Contraception* (Chicago, 1976); cf. my own *Sex, Love and Procreation* (Chicago, 1976) and "Contraception, Abstinence, and Responsible Parenthood," *Faith and Reason* 3 (1977) 34-52. It is significant, I believe, that with the exception of O'Reilly all the authors noted here are married laypeople.

68. On this Paul Marx, "Contraception: The Gateway," *International Review of Natural Family Planning* 1.3 (Fall, 1977) 276-279; see also R.S.J. Simpson, "Contraception: The Camel's Nose," *ibid.* 236-237. See also James V. Schall, *Human Dignity and Human Numbers* (New York, 1971).

69. A. Kosnik, et al. *Human Sexuality: New Directions in American Catholic Thought*. Kosnik and his colleagues reject as "too extrinsic and legal" the view that "every genital act outside the context of marriage is immoral" and develop a rationale that would even justify bestiality. For a detailed analysis and critique of this work see W. E. May and J.F. Harvey, *On Understanding "Human Sexuality"* (Chicago, 1976).

CHAPTER FIVE

The Magisterium: Biblical and Pastoral Aspects

Most Reverend John F. Whealon

One year ago the televised show *Roots* made many Americans give thought to their own geneological origins. In parallel fashion, we Catholics, when gathering to discuss the magisterium, are going back to the origins, the tap root, of our faith. We are talking not about an optional or secondary aspect of the faith, but about that which in final analysis makes Catholics Catholic and separates Catholics from other Christians. Acceptance of the magisterium and assent to the magisterium is the identifying Catholic belief.

In a real sense magisterium is an identifying mark of the Catholic Church, and acceptance of the magisterium is an identifying mark of the Catholic. In this ecumenical age I have come to understand the different Christian communities as differing indeed in doctrine, but differing also according to where they place final ecclesial authority under Christ. For the Orthodox it is the Patriarchate; for the Episcopalians it was the *episcopoi* or bishops; for the Presbyterians, the presbytery; for the Congregationalists, the individual congregation; and for the Baptists, no authority exists above the individual Christian. But for Catholics, as Section 25 of the *Dogmatic Constitution on the Church* of the Second Vatican Council teaches, final authority under Christ is found in the Pope and bishops, just as in the New Testament it reposed in Peter and the Apostles.

The importance of this for the ecumenical dialogue is evident. Historically, various Christian groups separated themselves from the Catholic Church because of theological or political reasons or a combination of both. The separation entailed a new authority under Christ. The challenge of the ecumenical dialogues, therefore, is to face both the theological questions and finally the authority question — which of course is profoundly, totally theological. And the resolution of the authority question, of the magisterium issue, will be the ultimate hurdle and will bring with it the resolution of the other dogmatic differences.

For this reason I am concerned about an AP press release, dated last December 28, reporting that representatives of the Roman Catholic and Episcopal Churches in the United States said "they've found basic unity between them and now want directives for further steps to take." The joint dialogue group, said the article, summarized the results of 19 meetings over 12 years, concluded that the representatives have found "a significant and substantial unity between the two Churches," asked for further direction and mandate from the two sponsoring bodies, and identified four "problem areas" needing further investigation by the sponsoring Churches. Those "problem areas" were listed as (1) authority in the Church, including the role of Pope and bishops; (2) the role of women; (3) the relationship between normative tradition and the individual conscience; (4) a study of the degree of unity necessary for sacramental sharing.

That which concerns me is that these doctrinal issues seem to be given equal weight, with authority regarded as simply another unresolved problem. In my judgment authority is in a certain sense the key issue in the total ecumenical dialogue, so that resolution of the issue of authority under Christ is that which will solve any other unresolved problems, which will make possible and even imperative our sacramental unity, and without which other agreements are only preliminary steps—beautiful and commendable steps indeed—towards the goal of Christian unity we must pray for and continue to seek.

In Catholic life and thinking today no topic is more important than the magisterium. For any priest or lay Catholic there is hardly any subject more alive, timely and helpful. Yet considering the importance of the magisterium for Catholic identity and unity, not enough has been written on it. Some contemporary catechetics seems not even to know the belief and seems therefore to lose Catholic identity in favor of a vague Christian Church with a Pope and bishops. How beneficial, therefore, to Catholics is a Symposium on the magisterium and its place and benefits in Catholic belief and life.

In this presentation I speak of magisterium or the teaching authority in the Catholic Church. I am thinking not of the rarely exercised infallible extraordinary magisterium, exercised when the Holy Father—with or without the college of bishops—solemnly defines a dogma of faith. I am speaking rather of the ordinary magisterium, the day-to-day admittedly reformable teaching of the Bishop of Rome, of the episcopate, or of the local diocesan bishop in union with the Pope.[1] The ordinary magisterium presumes that the Pope and bishops are in relationship with God's Word and are in dialogue with all voices in the Church, but are possessed of a special authority by reason of their ordained position in the Lord's Church.

The magisterium question is whether there exists in the Catholic Church an authority which ultimately by its authority obligates a Catholic to accept a teaching which that Catholic is not logically or psychologically disposed to accept. One recent example is the 1838 Constitution of Pope Gregory XVI, repeating papal teaching that slavery is immoral and that blacks are equal to whites in human dignity and rights (DS 2745-6).[2] This magisterial teaching, now universally accepted, was rejected by those who held that the Negro had no soul and could be subjected to slavery. A second example is the magisterial teaching of Pius XI in *Casti Connubii* (1929),[3] teaching that contraception is immoral. This teaching, essentially restated by the Second Vatican Council (1965)[4] and by Paul VI in *Humanae Vitae* (1968),[5] was rejected in its restatement by some Catholics who held that contraception is not intrinsically evil.[6] A more recent example is the magisterial teaching on the intrinsic evil of abortion.[7] Though generally accepted by Catholics, even this doctrine is rejected by a few Catholics. One Catholic author stated, "I find myself impatient with Catholic officialdom, which armors itself with rigorous logic in defense of unborn life —yet qualifies and equivocates on human life in so-called 'just wars.'"[8] In 1971 the Holy Father approved a curial statement making First Penance normative before First Communion[9]—and dissent has not yet ended. In 1976 the Sacred Congregation for the Doctrine of the Faith released a *Declaration on Certain Questions Concerning Sexual Ethics,*[10] approved by Pope Paul VI. The document presented traditional Catholic doctrine concerning premarital sex, living together without marriage, homosexual relations, masturbation, mortal sin and the ideal of chastity. The secular press gave generous coverage to Catholics, especially theologians, who publicly criticized this document.[11] In 1977 there was released a Curial statement, approved by the Pope, that the ordination of women cannot be authorized according to Catholic tradition[12]—and dissent was heard,[13] though muted. And in 1977 the book *Human Sexuality,*[14] written by Catholic theologians and actually subsidized by the Catholic Theological Society, publicly undermined both magisterial teaching on human sexuality and the very bases for that teaching.

These examples illustrate the problem of the magisterium for many contemporary Catholics. Is there in the Catholic Church an authority which ultimately by its authority alone obligates a Catholic to accept a teaching which that Catholic logically or psychologically really doesn't want to accept? To search out the answer we must look at the Biblical evidence first. And the New Testament has something to say on authority in the Church—the authority of the apostles; the special authority of Peter. Let me indicate this briefly: from the New Testament comes a conviction that the ultimate authority and the one authoritative Teacher is Jesus our Master. Also from the New Testament comes our belief that the Master gave teaching authority to Peter and the other apostles. The word authority holds the root *augere:* it is solely (as Robert Grosseteste[15] said) to increase or build up the Church. The exercise of this authority is a service, in Christ and for the Body of Christ. Also from the New Testament comes the lesson that Peter had a dominant authority in teaching. Mark's Gospel, as Peter's *didache,* was the foundation of the other Gospels. Cephas (Peter) influenced Paul also, stood first on the list of the apostles and had the normative teaching. From Paul we get the picture that is essentially the concept of magisterium: there were and are false apostles and false teachers, but agreement with Cephas was and is the norm of Christian orthodoxy.[16]

The major texts testifying to the magisterial office of Peter and the apostles are Matthew, Chapter 16—the chapter in which the human weakness of Peter is stressed, along with Christ's promise to make Peter the foundation of the Church and keeper of the keys of heaven; and also John 21, undoubtedly the last Gospel material to be written down, in which the Church recalled how the risen Lord appointed Peter to be Shepherd of the Lord's entire flock, with love for Christ as the precondition to the appointment. I consider the New Testament evidence for the authority of Peter and the apostles to be clear and convincing. One indeed can challenge the way in which this concept developed in the Catholic Church or has been exercised at various periods of history. Those are real questions, indeed — but questions that should not obscure the Biblical evidence. Theologically, the doctrine on the ordinary magisterium is presented in Chapter Three of the *Constitution on the Church*. This chapter begins with the teaching that the successor of Peter and the successors of the apostles — the Pope and the bishops — have inherited the responsibility and service in the Church that is magisterium.

The key text for understanding the ordinary magisterium is paragraph 25 of the *Constitution on the Church*.

> Bishops, teaching in communion with the Roman Pontiff, are to be respected by all as witnesses to divine and Catholic truth. In matters of faith and morals, the bishops speak in the name of Christ and the faithful are to accept their teaching and adhere to it with a religious assent of soul. This religious submission of will and of mind must be shown in a special way to the authentic teaching authority of the Roman Pontiff, even when he is not speaking ex cathedra. That is, it must be shown in such a way that his supreme magisterium is acknowledged with reverence, the judgments made by him are sincerely adhered to, according to his manifest mind and will. His mind and will in the matter may be known chiefly either from the character of the documents, from his frequent repetition of the same doctrine, or from his manner of speaking.

I see this text as saying that the members of the Lord's flock are in doctrinal matters to follow the one appointed as Shepherd of the entire flock. Organizationally the Church's teaching authority is an immeasurable service to the entire Church. A Catholic can know what the Church teaches. Even when the question is a particularly controverted one, the Catholic need have no doubt concerning Catholic doctrine.

Psychologically, the very idea of magisterium is not well received in an age when all authority is challenged. The word magisterium comes from *magister* or "master." For us in the United States the master is one who dominates. We have lost the meaning, still found in England, of the master as the teacher. There is a certain tension in this, because magisterial teaching is teaching given with the authority of a teacher. The authority in the magisterium, however, comes not from the person but rather from the doctrine and the office. It must be teaching given in the name of Christ, in the Spirit of Truth. And the correlative to *magister* is *minister*. The spokesmen of this Teaching of Christ are themselves subservient to it.

In this modern age there is a resistance to the inescapable intellectual humility, docility, openness to acceptance which magisterium demands. As teachers today testify, too few seem willing to learn. But a teacher makes no sense, functionally and philosophically, unless there are learners. There can be no *docentes* without *discentes*. Conceit and presumption cause special problems here, as the German bishops have noted. We do not like to be considered sheep of the Lord's and Peter's flock. So psychologically the magisterium does not now receive an open reception, a fair hearing.

A further problem for the magisterium is its very name. "Magisterium" sounds foreign, oppressive, heavy. The expression "teaching authority" is more palatable. However this is a concept not to be sold by advertising. Perhaps it is good that we see this, in all its Roman bluntness, as no easy pill to swallow.

The magisterial aspect of the Catholic Church is indeed its least attractive feature. In Vatican II's masterwork, *The Constitution on the Church,* Chapter Two describes the Church as the People of God. This chapter is a fresh, attractive, biblically-based presentation of the Church. This chapter is a pleasure to read and to present to others through instruction and homily. But the next chapter of that same document is dramatically different in spirit. Chapter Three, treating the hierarchy and the magisterium of the Church, is theological, canonical, formal. Chapter Three is hardly attractive for teaching or preaching.

That Chapter Three is something like the skeleton of the Mystical Body. No beauty is there, especially when isolated or dissected. Yet like a skeleton it performs an essential function in the Church. So this unappealing concept of the operative ordinary magisterium is, intellectually speaking, a critical question in today's Church for the priest and for many laity.

Historically the concept of magisterium needs, it seems to me, a far more searching and sympathetic interpretation than it has generally received. As was indicated earlier in this paper, I am speaking of the admittedly reformable magisterial teaching of the Church, and not of its rare, irreformable, infallible teaching. Yet so often the reformable magisterium is criticized because it has been reformed, because in subsequent times with changing conditions and greater wisdom a previous teaching was seen as erroneous or inadequate and in need of correction. There is, in regard to the fallible magisterium, an excessive expectation that it too must be always infallible. Too many share Faber's view that the

Pope should be understood "as if heaven were always open over his head and the light shone down upon him" and that opposition to him was the sin against the Holy Spirit. Too many still would like an infallible statement at the breakfast table each morning with their copy of the *London Times*.

The usual objections against a revisionist magisterium are teachings on usury, the Galileo incident, Popes who had personal problems from politics or sex or worldliness. Back of the objections are erroneous expectations that the successors of St. Peter must always be perfect and that their teachings and practices must always be perfect. The concept of the ordinary magisterium is however one of the safe and prudent guidance of the shepherd in matters of faith and morals — but a guidance that is open to improvement and even correction if greater wisdom comes.

It is helpful to note how the theologian John Henry Newman regarded the magisterium. A Catholic parent asked Newman if her son might enroll at Oxford University, even though a rescript from the Holy See had cautioned Catholics against attending Oxford or Cambridge. Newman replied: "Whether the Pope be infallible or not (Newman's words were written before the definition of papal infallibility), in any pronouncement he is to be obeyed.... His facts and his warning may all be wrong. His deliberations may have been biased. He may have been misled. Imperiousness and craft, tyranny and cruelty may be patent in the conduct of his advisers and instruments. But when he speaks formally and authoritatively, he speaks as Our Lord would have him speak, and all these imperfections are overruled for the result which Our Lord intends...."[17]

Probably the most complete change in magisterial teaching is that which has taken place since 1964 in regard to Biblical Studies. In 1902, Pope

Leo XIII issued the Apostolic Letter *Vigilantiae*,[18] establishing a Commission for Biblical Studies to give direction in Biblical studies according to the norms of Biblical scholarship and Catholic doctrine. In 1907 Pope Pius X made the decisions of the Biblical Commission binding.[19] That Commission, starting in times of Modernism, upheld the general historicity of the books of Holy Scripture[20] and the Mosaic authorship of the Pentateuch[21]; stated that the Apostle John and no other authored the Fourth Gospel,[22] that there was one author of Isaiah,[23] that Paul wrote the Pastorals[24] and Hebrews.[25] In 1943, however, Pope Pius XII issued *Divino Afflante Spiritu*, mandating attention to literary forms in the Bible.[26] In April of 1964 the Pontifical Biblical Commission issued its latest decree,[27] mandating a study of the Gospels as developing through three states of composition. That 1964 Decree, with the 1965 *Constitution on Revelation* of the Second Vatican Council, effectively reversed and superseded all the earlier Decrees of the Pontifical Biblical Commission[28] (as the Secretary had said[29]), and turned Catholics away from fundamentalism and to an open scientific study of the Sacred Scriptures. With the knowledge of the 1970's we could easily criticize those early Biblical Commission decrees. But such criticism would be both unfair and cheap. We should rather express contentment that we have a magisterium that is reformable and flexible.

The question here is delicate and complex. I know of no wiser treatment than that of the German bishops in a pastoral letter of September 22, 1967. The pastoral says:

> At this point we must soberly discuss a difficult question, which in the case of many Catholics today, much more than in the past, either menaces their faith or their spontaneous confidence in the doctrinal authority of the Church. We are thinking of the fact that in the exercise of its office, the doctrinal authority of the Church can be subject to error and has in fact erred.

The Church has always known that something of the
sort was possible. It has stated it in its theology and
developed rules for such situations. This possibility of
error does not affect doctrines which are proclaimed to
be held with absolute assent, by a solemn definition
of the Pope or of a General Council or by the ordinary
magisterium. It is also historically wrong to affirm that
errors of the Church have subsequently been discovered in such dogmas. This of course is not to deny that
in the case of a dogma growth in understanding is always possible and always necessary, the original sense
being maintained while previous possible minunder-
standings are eliminated. And of course the problem in
question must not be confused with the obvious fact
that there is changeable human law in the Church as
well as divine and unalterable law. Changes in such
human law have nothing to do with error, but simply
raise the question of the opportuneness of legal disposi-
tions at different times. As regards error and the possibility of error in non-defined doctrinal pronouncements
of the Church, where in fact the degree of obligation
can vary very widely, we must begin by accepting
soberly and resolutely the fact that the whole of our
human life in general has also to be lived simply
"according to the best of our knowledge." We have to
follow our conscience according to our lights, which
cannot be justified with absolute intellectual certainty
but still remain "here and now" the valid norms to be
respected in thought and action, because for the present
there is nothing better. This is something which everyone knows from his own experience. It is a truth accepted by every doctor in his diagnosis and by every
statesman in his judgment of a political situation and
the decisions to be taken in view of it. The Church too,
in its doctrine and practice, cannot always allow itself
to be faced by the dilemma of either giving an abso-
lutely binding doctrinal decision or simply remaining
silent and leaving everything to the personal opinion
of the individual. To safeguard the real substance of
the faith, the Church must give doctrinal instructions,
which have a certain degree of obligation but, not being
definitions of the faith, have a certain provisional
character, even to the extent of possible error. This is
a risk which must be taken, since otherwise the Church
would find it quite impossible to preach its faith as
the decisive reality of life, to expound it and to apply

it to each new situation of man. In such a case, the situation of the individual with regard to the Church is somewhat like that of a man who knows that he is bound to accept the decision of an expert, even though he knows that this is not infallible.

There is no place, at any rate, in sermons and religious instruction for opinions contrary to such provisional doctrinal pronouncements of the Church, even though in certain circumstances the faithful should have the nature and the limited scope of such provisional pronouncements explained to them.... The Christian who believes he has a right to his private opinion, that he already knows what the Church will only come to grasp later, must ask himself in sober self-criticism before God and his conscience, whether he has the necessary depth and breadth of theological expertise to allow his private theory and practice to depart from the present doctrine of the ecclesiastical authorities. The case is in principle admissible. But conceit and presumption will have to answer for their willfulness before the judgment-seat of God.

The magisterium has had a more difficult time since 1962 because of the extraordinary publicity given to any theologian or theologians who challenged or dissented from the magisterium. Most of the Catholic faithful are able to know what the Pope and bishops teach. But most of the faithful are not equipped to respond personally to the complex dogmatic or moral points made by a dissenting theologian. As a result the faithful are confused.

There is also the danger of undue influence from the pressures of current popular opinion and propaganda. Authentic magisterium has been entrusted exclusively to the bishops as successors of the Apostles in union with Peter's successor. There is no place for a paramagisterium in the Lord's flock.

This present difficulty, in my judgment, dates back to 1962. Pope John XXIII convened Vatican II as a pastoral, eirenic Council. It issued no anathemas. Its spirit was that eloquently described by Pope John in his opening address. The Pope said that the Council must defend and advance truth, but that it should take a non-condemnatory posture towards error. He said: "We see, in fact, as one age succeeds another, that the opinions of men follow one another and exclude each other. And often errors vanish as quickly as they arise, like fog before the sun. The Church has always opposed these errors. Frequently she has condemned them with the greatest severity. Nowadays, however, the spouse of Christ prefers to make use of the medicine of mercy rather than that of severity. She considers that she meets the needs of the present day by demonstrating the validity of her teaching rather than by condemnations." [30]

The Index of Prohibited Books has been abolished.[31] The standards for the *imprimatur* have been reduced.[32] Some theologians blithely advocate publicly teaching contrary to the clearly expressed doctrine of the magisterium. The Holy See, following the medicine of mercy, reiterates its teachings, tries to have them more widely and clearly understood, but takes only reluctant and indirect action against dissenters, with utmost respect for human dignity. The reasons, I think, are a pastoral and magisterial solicitude for reconciling the dissenters, combined with a prudential judgment that in the long run the Church has more to lose than to gain by severe measures. But the price we are paying is some confusion as to what "the Church teaches" because some do not know the authentic teachers in the Church.

I should like to conclude with practical observations concerning the attitude of a bishop, priest, deacon and lay person towards magisterial teaching.

How should anyone in Holy Orders think and speak when faced with a magisterial teaching which he does not understand or does not like or does not accept?

Certainly every priest, deacon and bishop must look upon self as a *man of the Church*. Such are, indeed, men of Christ. But every Christian is expected to be another Christ. That which sets ordained ministers apart from the others is the Sacrament of Orders. Those in Orders are placed in special relationship to Christ, and in particular relationship to the Church. They become ministers *of the Church* to the rest of God's people. They are not their own. They are men of the Church.

Recently there has been considerable obscuring of the understanding by priests of themselves as Churchmen. During the past ten years bishops have been made to feel occasionally almost isolated from priests and priest groups – as if somehow an adversary relationship exists between bishops and priests, so that a bishop must defend before priests the teachings of the Church. The unity of the presbyterium is important. And that unity will be stronger when bishops and priests sense themselves as united in Holy Orders and priestly ministry, together men of the Church. Certainly the relationship is never to be one of management vs. labor, with a Senate of Priests acting as an adversary labor union.

Considering self a man of the Church means considering self a man of Chapter Three of the *Constitution on the Church* – as a part of the hierarchy – as well as of Chapter Two. As that Chapter Three states: "Priests, prudent cooperators with the episcopal order as well as its aids and instruments, are called to serve the People of God. They constitute one priesthood with their bishop.... Associated with their bishop in a spirit of trust and generosity, priests make him present in a certain sense in the individual local congregation of the faithful...."[33]

A second expectation is that the priest – as well as the bishop and deacon – will teach and preach as the Church's doctrine only that which the magisterium has presented as the Church's doctrine. As men and ministers of the Church they are fully expected to present the Church's teachings — and not their own ideas or speculations, or the ideas and speculations of theologians *qua* theologians. This point — which is expectation of the official and the general Church — is of paramount importance. The neglect of this principle has led to enormous confusion in the minds of the laity and some priests.

The entire concept of faculties to preach and teach illustrates how the spokesman for the Church must present the Church's doctrine. The bishop cannot give faculties to one who does not preach or teach the Church's doctrine.

What are the expectations for the laity? How can the laity know what is the official teaching of the Church on a question of faith or morals? That doctrine is easily learned, especially in this age of rapid communications. A rule of thumb for the Catholic laity is to accept the teaching of a deacon or priest if he is in agreement with the local bishop, and to accept the teaching of the local bishop if he is in agreement with the Pope. And for a priest the rule of thumb is even more simple. The priest (or deacon) follows the teaching of his bishop if that worthy is in concert with the Pope, and in every final instance he follows the Pope. It is now as it was in New Testament times: Cephas is the norm for our doctrine; unity with Peter's successor is essential. The Petrine office is our guarantee of unity of faith and doctrine. And with modern communications so effective, no deacon or priest, no bishop or lay person need long doubt as to what is Catholic teaching.

What of the priest who does not reflect or express the official Church teaching in his public or private utterances? Here precisely is the cause of confusion. The simple Catholic trusts the priest and rightly expects that a priest would not teach a doctrine at variance with that of the local bishop or the Pope. Yet Frank Sheed, that doughty theologian and student of the Catholic scene, writes that "there is hardly a doctrine or practice of the Church I have not heard attacked by a priest" [34] (*Is It the Same Church?*, p. xiv). Small wonder that there has been widespread confusion in the minds of Catholic faithful. The duty of us ministers of the Church, particularly ordained ones, is to present publicly the Church's teaching, the whole Church's teaching and (as formal doctrine) nothing but the Church's teaching, so help us God.

The *Encyclopedia of Theology* expresses well the need for a modern understanding of magisterium: "In spite of the individualism of later days, which is still very much the prevailing temper of the West, a new understanding for the magisterium of the Church must surely now be possible, in view of our knowledge of the man of today and tomorrow. Man cannot possess his truth as an isolated individual, since he is no such thing.... But in a post-individualistic epoch new possibilities of understanding may be opened up, even for the understanding of the magisterium of the Church." [35] A better understanding of the Church's magisterium is indeed imperative for many contemporary Catholics. Until that better understanding is reached, confusion will continue.

Any Catholic who does not follow the teaching and direction planned by Christ, given by the Pope and the bishops united with him, is left only with personal opinion of self or others. That Catholic is crossing Niagara Falls on a tightrope and not on the bridge built by the Pontifex. For such a Catholic the key has been discarded, the sheep has no shepherd, the net does not enfold and there is no assured witness to the genuine Christ.

The magisterium, an enormous gift to the Church, is by the design of Christ there to give guidance and bring peace of mind. And we need the magisterium even more in this questioning, challenging, publicity-conscious, changing modern society.

Footnotes

1. *Lumen Gentium*, paragraph 25.
2. H. Denzinger, A. Schönmetzer, *Enchiridion Symbolorum Definitionum et Declarationum de Rebus Fidei et Morum*, 35th ed. (Freiburg im Breisgau, 1973) n. 2745 f. (from now on simply *DS*).
3. *Acta Apostolicae Sedis* 22 (1930) 541-592.
4. *Gaudium et Spes*, n. 51.
5. *Acta Apostolicae Sedis* 60 (1968) 480-503.
6. Ample documentation is given in Dr. May's paper.
7. Declaration of the Sacred Congregation for the Doctrine of the Faith of November 18, 1974, *Acta Apostolicae Sedis* 66 (1974) 730-747.
8. M.C. Segars, "Abortion: The Last Resort," *America* 133 (1975) 456.
9. Sacred Congregation for the Clergy, *General Catechetical Directory* (Washington, 1971) 98-103.
10. Declaration of the Sacred Congregation for the Doctrine of the Faith of December 29, 1975, *Acta Apostolicae Sedis* 68 (1976) 77-96.
11. For much of the reaction, see R. McCormick, "Notes on Moral Theology," *Theological Studies* 38 (1977) 101-112.
12. Declaration of the Sacred Congregation for the Doctrine of the Faith of October 15, 1976, *Acta Apostolicae Sedis* 69 (1977) 96-116.
13. See, e.g., statement by Woman's Ordination Conference in *Origins: NC Documentary Service* 6 (1976/77) 545.
14. A. Kosnic, et al., *Human Sexuality: New Directions in Catholic Thought* (New York, 1977).
15. Bishop of Lincoln from 1235 until 1253 who participated in Council of Lyons I in 1245.
16. R. Brown, K. Donfried, J. Reumann, *Peter in the New Testament: A Collaborative Assessment by Protestant and Roman Catholic Scholars* Minneapolis, 1973) *passim*.
17. "Letter to Lady Simeon" of November 10, 1867 in C.S. Dessain, T. Gornall, edd., *The Letters and Diaries of John Henry Newman*, vol. XXIII (Oxford, 1973) 365f.
18. *Enchiridion Biblicum*, 3rd ed. (Naples and Rome, 1956) n. 137-148.
19. *Enchiridion Biblicum* n. 283-288.
20. *Enchiridion Biblicum* n. 161.
21. *Enchiridion Biblicum* n. 181-184.
22. *Enchiridion Biblicum* n. 187.
23. *Enchiridion Biblicum* n. 294.
24. *Enchiridion Biblicum* n. 412-414.
25. *Enchiridion Biblicum* n. 416-417.
26. *Enchiridion Biblicum* n. 558-560.
27. *Acta Apostolicae Sedis* 56 (1964) 712-718.
28. *Dei Verbum*, especially chapters 3-5.
29. A. Miller in *Benedictinische Monatschrift* 31 (1955) 49f.; see also the words of the then Undersecretary of the Pontifical Biblical Commission in *Antonianum* 30 (1955) 63ff.

30. Translation found in W. Abbott, gen. ed., *The Documents of Vatican II* (New York, 1966) 715f.

31. Notification of the Sacred Congregation for the Doctrine of the Faith of June 14, 1966 in *Acta Apostolicae Sedis* 58 (1966) 445.

32. Decree of the Sacred Congregation for the Doctrine of the Faith of November 15, 1966 in *Acta Apostolicae Sedis* 58, 1186. Matters have been made more stringent recently; see Decree of the Sacred Congregation for the Doctrine of the Faith of March 19, 1975 in *Acta Apostolicae Sedis* 67 (1975) 281-284.

33. *Lumen Gentium*, paragraph 28.

34. F. Sheed, *Is It the Same Church?* (Dayton, 1969) xiv.

35. K. Rahner, "Magisterium" in K. Rahner, ed., *Encyclopedia of Theology: The Concise Sacramentum Mundi* (New York, 1975) 873.

CHAPTER SIX

The Magisterium and Catholic Higher Education

Most Reverend Jeremiah Newman
Bishop of Limerick, Ireland

Introduction

I am most appreciative of the honor which has been done me by inviting me to take part in this important Symposium and I only hope that my contribution will be found useful.

The subject on which I have been asked to speak is "The Magisterium and Catholic Higher Education." I am glad to get an opportunity to say something on this subject.

To be sure, I am conscious of the difficulties in my way, the difficulty of avoiding overlapping with other papers at this meeting and that of saying anything new at all in the matter.

For all this has been a much debated area for some years now—at such forums as congresses of the International Federation of Catholic Universities, the Conference on Catholic Higher Education held in New York in 1973, the Meeting of European Bishops of October, 1975, also the congresses held under the auspices of the Congregation for Catholic Education in Rome in 1972 and again in 1976. However, I am hopeful that I may have something of value to add to all this discussion.

An essential prerequisite is to endeavor to define exactly the terms in the title of my paper— "The Magisterium and Catholic Higher Education."

First of all, there is the meaning of "Magisterium." As in the case of so many other terms and concepts that were one time taken for granted, this has now become rigorously subjected to the techniques of linguistic and logical analysis. While its implications have already been teased out in other papers delivered here, for my purposes I cannot find a better treatment of these than that contained in the lecture delivered by Bishop Robert Coffy to the Meeting of European Bishops in 1975.

I quote: "It could be necessary to commission a study of the term 'Magisterium.' Up to Pius IX it seems that the word meant authority in general. During the nineteenth century it acquired the specific meaning of doctrinal authority and this happened in a given historical context in which faith was seen as, above all, intellectual acquiesence to a body of truths. And thus emerged a limitation of the meaning of the concept of Magisterium. This now had the function of watching over the rectitude of the formulation of the faith. In a form closer to the truth, the faith is today presented as an assent of the whole being to the Mystery of Salvation.... This means that the truths of faith are no longer considered as mere conceptual constructs. They must tie up with the experiences and with the deeper aspirations of men.... By placing the Magisterium in this frame of understanding the faith, we offer it a function which spans and embraces deeper and wider realities. The ministry of the Magisterium then, does not only seek the right expressions of the faith but also the right way of praying, of behaving, of living the faith.... In this way the ministry of the Magisterium is not reduced to safeguarding doctrinal rectitude (orthodoxy) but extended to guarding over-practical righteousness (orthopraxis), as in the celebration of the faith (liturgy)." [1]

From this point of view of understanding the Magisterium, there is no great importance in a distinction between a "doctrinal" and a "pastoral"

Magisterium and in practice it means that the Magisterium is to be understood as meaning "authority over faith and morals and the general practice of the faith."

The second term in the title to my paper which has to be defined is "Education." Here it is necessary to make a distinction between education as "teaching" and education as "research." As teaching, education is the handing on of any particular subject matter by way of a formative, conservative influence. As research, it is the scientific investigation of any such subject matter, a pushing forward towards new horizons, a deepening of grasp of its content.

Thirdly, there is "Catholic" education. Here again a distinction is necessary between education in secular subjects under a Catholic aegis (for example, chemistry, civil law and the like) and education in religious subjects under the same aegis (that is, Catholic doctrinal teaching and Catholic theological research).

Lastly, we have "Higher" education. As in the case of the previous two terms, a distinction is also called for here—between third level educational institutions, including seminaries and other-than-universities and faculties on the one hand, and universities and faculties on the other, whether formally Catholic or civil.

For the purpose of this paper I shall limit myself to dealing with the relationship of the Magisterium to Catholic Higher Education in the sense of all third level education—whether in universities, seminaries or elsewhere—that is devoted to either the teaching of Catholic doctrine (say Catholic theology for short) or the advancement of Catholic theological research in the widest sense of that term, including therefore Sacred Scripture and all sciences directly allied to theology. I am only too well aware that anything that I may say in this matter has implications for Catholic education at every level.

The Question

The question which I shall pose is twofold. On the one hand, what precisely should be the relations between Catholic educators (whether teachers or researchers) and the Magisterium? On the other hand, what precisely should be the stance of the Magisterium towards problems which may arise in the matter of these relations?

Both of these questions boil down ultimately and very quickly to the extent and nature of the academic freedom of doctrinal teaching and theological research in Catholic higher education and how this should be handled in cases of conflict. This indeed has been evident now for quite a number of years. It is interesting to note that the question of academic freedom is not confined to Catholic educators. It has arisen also in general educational institutions as regards secular subjects. Witness to this is provided in such books as Professor Sydney Hook's *In Defence of Academic Freedom* (published in New York as far back as 1971) or the contribution of Professor Robert Paul Wolff of Columbia to the book *The University Crisis Reader* (also published in 1971). It is interesting to note too that this new concern about academic freedom is but one facet of a wider concern in our time about "political" freedoms of all kinds. In witness to this we again have Professor Hook's other book, *The Paradoxes of Freedom* (1962), and Professor Wolff's *In Defence of Anarchism* (1970).

And, whereas the question of academic freedom in secular subjects has come to be taken up by such organs of opinion as the American Civil Liberties Union, through canvassing in places like its handbook, *The Rights of Teachers* (New York 1972), that of Catholic educators as such is being examined on platforms such as those afforded by the meetings of the F.I.U.C., the aforementioned congresses at Rome or the present symposium.

It is well for us to recognize the contemporary historical dimension of this because it will help us to realize that, like so many other problems which agitate the Church at present, it is the product of a time-conditioned situation.

As I have often adverted to on other occasions, this only underlies the human aspect of the Church — subject to the stresses and strains of society in general ⟵ which in truth it is well to underline, in view of so-called humanist assertions to the contrary. Grace works always through nature.

But to return to the central question of this paper, namely, the role of the Magisterium in respect of Catholic Higher Education, it should be remembered that, since the Council, there have been certain developments. Whereas formerly the exclusively accepted method of theology was what is termed the "regressive" method, i.e., that of quoting magisterial pronouncements and then seeking scriptural and patristic justification for them, now the method is what is sometimes called "genetic," i.e., working from scripture and tradition and the declarations of the Magisterium towards a rounded exposition of any doctrinal question.

Nevertheless, difficulties remain on the part of some Catholic educators, notably certain theologians, who would seem to wish for complete freedom in the pursuit of religious truth, a freedom entirely untrammelled by magisterial utterances. This is especially true in the field of theological research.

The Approach

I do not propose to approach this matter from either the theological or magisterial standpoint. To do so might appear to be prejudiced or at least seem to beg the question. To take up an attitude based on assumptions related to a science of theology as a self-contained discipline, with the Magisterium as a kind of foreign body pertaining to a different sphere, could indeed end up onesided. Equally, to fall back on a traditional concept of the Magisterium and its traditional ways of acting could be both unconvincing and fail to be seen as an objective and just method of treating the question.

As one whose personal intellectual formation has been mainly in the field of philosophy and the human sciences, I shall endeavor rather to draw from these fields some insights relating to education both as teaching and research and to try to use these for the purpose of throwing some light on the subject at issue.

It may be surprising to many to say that, basically, I regard the problem as one of politics. Yes, but of "politics" in the purest sense of the word. I have come to this conclusion as a result of reading David J. Bell's book, *Power, Influence and Authority* (1975). The thesis of this book is based on a redefinition of politics, centering on the three terms of its title, or rather on the interaction of the three forces which these three terms represent. As thus expounded, the relationships between parents and children, teachers and pupils, even friends and acquaintances are "political" (and so therefore also between the Magisterium and Catholic educators).

For Bell politics is talk—power talk, influence talk, authority talk. It takes many forms. "Notice," he says, "how many different styles of talk we use, our voice level, and even the content of our conversation to the 'situation.' Thus we have 'pillow talk,' 'small talk,' 'cocktail conversation,' 'shop talk,' 'sweet talk,' and so on. We scold children for 'talking back' to their parents. We bristle when someone 'talks sharply' to another, perhaps expecting a reply in 'fighting words.' Governments generate their own linguistic categories, including 'strong talk,' 'election

talk,' 'testimony,' 'formal statement,' 'official comment,' 'diplomatic talk,' 'negotiation'...." and so on.[2]
    I think it is fair to say that religious education is
also talk—by the giver to the receiver—and that it can
and has taken all these forms of "political" talk, that
is, power talk, influence talk and authority talk. So
too are the statements and reactions of the Church's
Magisterium. As a result, in the sense in which I am
speaking of politics here, the problem of my paper is
reduced to a political one.
    Against this background, let me take a brief look
at education as both teaching and research, with
particular application to the subject "The Magisterium and Catholic Higher Education."

Education as Teaching

    Teaching (pedagogy if you like) is the first func-
tion of all education. It has been said that nobody has
defined education better than the Brazilian writer
Paulo Freire, who describes the educational process
as a becoming critically aware of one's reality in a
manner which leads to effective action upon it.[3]
While there is a great deal of truth in this, it would
still appear that the most fundamental and prior
process of education is that of socialization, the socialization of one's reality as a whole, so as to be
able to act on society from within, avoid being an
a priori outsider, avoid in fact an anarchical position.
    This holds for one's reality in all one's social
being, whether that of the family, the local community, industry and commerce, the State and also
the Church. And it involves multiple and complex
experiences.
    In accordance with my reference to politics in
relation to the subject of this paper, take political
socialization in the most obvious sense. It is accepted
that such socialization is essentially the process
whereby political systems maintain themselves

against breakdown or over-radical change. In other words, it places stress on the conservative task of transmitting appropriate attitudes from generation to generation. Various agencies are involved in this: domestic influences, the school, the mass media and the like. In one way or another all are expected to inculcate an awareness of belonging to a particular community and a loyalty to it.

As far as the individual person is concerned, this entails a development from early engendered feelings as regards preferences and views to mature thinking about a body of acquired information — in other words, a growth from non-cognitive to cognitive participation.[4]

What is evident in all this process is the role which "system support" plays in it, the role, that is, of such things as family concern, school ethos, media policy, etc. In regard to the whole, there is an evident need to try to effect a balance between conservation and innovation, an acceptance of the necessity of cognitive integration into the system before any meaningful reaction upon it is possible. In short, the inculcation of generally accepted positions is the first element of all education.

The Church is not excluded from this process. Rather should I say that it is confronted with somewhat the same kind of problem as that of political socialization in the strict sense.

I have said "somewhat" the same kind of problem, because there is a greater limit to "cognitive deviance" in respect of the acceptance of basic religious beliefs. The fundamental reason for this is the lesser choice which is open in the Church to options, such as democracy, that are available in secular political society. In the Church we are presented with a hierarchically ordered system and a body of faith and morals, which are preconditions of membership of it at all. In other words, irrespective of what one may like to think, there are certain things which one has always to accept if one is to retain participation in the Catholic "ecclesiological polity." There is all the difference in the world between this and the wide spectrum of choices that is open in the domain of "secular polity."

Programmed Learning

In consequence of this, Catholic education at all levels has perforce to fall into the category of what is currently described as "programmed" education or learning.[5]

It is now about twenty years since the advent of appreciation of this method. While originally derived from animal learning, it has now been extended to that of human. There is no adequate reason why it should not be so extended if, as has been properly remarked, the very complexity of human behavior may have obscured basic learning processes that are shared by lesser species. The whole thing comes back to whether one wants to impart a particular cognitive and behavioral response, the first goal of all education. It is of special relevance to the transmission of the belief and morality for which Christianity and Catholicism stands.

In the animal kingdom, the educator (trainer) has to try to communicate his goal by way of maneuvering his subject gradually towards it. With humans this is done by way of verbal instruction and explanation.

The big difference is that in the case of the former there is no question of any foreknowledge of what is intended, whereas in the latter it is to be assumed that the learner wishes to attain to the goal. Otherwise he would not be a learner at all.

As a learner, he must primarily at least be passive. It has been noted that, while one hears frequently about the importance of active student involvement in the learning process by way of input, educational

practice on the whole shows that such activity is
not an essential factor in the learning process as such.

I am reminded here of my time as President of
Maynooth when, during a period of unrest about
courses some ten years ago, much emphasis was
placed by students on the importance of their own
contribution to their theological formation. At one
stage in this interchange of views concerning sem-
inars as against lectures, I was driven to observe that
it seemed to some as if truth could be arrived at by
a democratic process of uninformed debate: "Hands
up those who are in favor of three persons rather
than one person in God"!

It should be seen clearly that the criterion for
the possession of knowledge of whatsoever kind is
the ability to express it — as in speech or writing —
and to adopt an appropriate model of behavior ac-
cordingly. Because of this, the educator should aim,
no matter what subject he may be teaching, to produce
cognitive acceptance and compatible criterion behavior as regards it.

This approach to learning, to wit, that the learner
will consistently make the correct responses to what
he is being taught, by reason of receiving definite
positive reinforcement of it, has been termed the
"linear" method in education. To be fair to it, it does
allow for the subsequent presentation of what, within
its framework, are considered "wrong" responses,
but only to the extent that these are always immediately countered by further and more elaborate
explanations of the "right" response.

There are some educators who maintain that a
programmed approach can be achieved within a
kind of intrinsic patterning which confronts the
learner with simultaneous multiple choice testing,
whereby a more open system of instruction is presented, with concomitant interjections as to why
particular responses are wrong. This has been termed

the "branching" method in education, the learner being faced with a number of alternative answers and asked to choose between them, albeit warned of the possibility of incorrect answers.

In my experience of Catholic higher education, I have, I believe, found this latter method followed in some quarters within ecumenical consortiums which pool both students and teachers for the imparting of Christian doctrine, with certain inbuilt mechanisms whereby the Catholic point of view is indicated to the Catholic students during or after lectures to them by non-Catholic teachers. While this is undoubtedly motivated by the highest considerations relating to ecumenical cooperation, I have my doubts as to whether it is the kind of programmed education that Catholic students—and in particular seminarians—should receive. Indeed it is hard to see how it can at all be termed programming in any realistic sense of the word.

Programmed learning takes place only with positive help at every stage. It is clear that alternatives can and should be put forward for the purpose of a full comprehension of issues by the student and the ensuring of a thoroughly enlightened mind. But "it is generally agreed that in a program as a whole the frequency of correct responses made should outweigh the wrong responses."

It is for this reason, I feel sure, that the Roman Congregation for Catholic Education, in its "Norms for Priestly Formation" and "The Theological Training of Future Priests," has specified the courses and content of studies to be pursued by seminarians. This in fact is what is meant, at least in part, as far as theological training is concerned, by the phrase "Systematic Theology."

A Supportive System

It is surely the task of teachers in Catholic higher education to carry out such a program. As teachers they are an integral part of the system support which Catholic education, like all education, requires. In propounding this view one might seem to be open to the charge of advocating a Soviet-type approach to education by way of control over educational institutions, teaching appointments, textbooks, syllabuses and so forth, through which students are exposed only to the official outlook and have little opportunity to hear or read anything else.

In this connection it should not be forgotten that, as has already been pointed out, system support is compatible with a controlled exposition of minority views. It is therefore compatible with the accomodation of elite groups who articulate critical attitudes within the received corpus. In the context of Catholic higher education this latter function pertains chiefly to the role of the educationalist as researcher of which I will say more later.

The upshot of what I am saying is that in the free world — including Church as well as State — education has to be geared to the primary purpose of ensuring compliance with the demands of society, while at the same time being free, within certain limits, to probe the possibility of development.

As I have also said, the scope for such development is more restricted in the Church than in civil society because of the very nature of the Church. It is therefore of vital importance that Catholic educational institutions at all levels seek to impart an intellectual and behavioral formation of the kind that is in harmony with genuine "Catholicity." Otherwise their teaching, to use the title of a well-known book, is only a form of "subversive activity."

It is simply not good enough for Catholic teachers to adopt a kind of airy-fairy approach to their task, putting non-commital views before their pupils, or worse leaving them to choose for themselves between a conglomeration of what are presented as Christian alternatives. Any true believer has to face up to the fact that he cannot be either equivocal or non-supportive in the matter of the transmission of his beliefs.

He cannot pretend that his role is not related to the possibility of attitude change on the part of his hearers. Attitudes in any sphere can change and there is now a large body of literature relating to the agents which can play a part in such change.[7] As far as change in religious attitudes goes, it has been wisely noted that one of the main conditions is a powerful and attractive new presentation of viewpoint. Sometimes this is effected by charismatic leaders, sometimes by other sources among which educators can be a prominent category.

One notable secular expert on education has put it as follows: "As in the case of science, common language, communication and commonly accepted standards of reason and logic are necessary conditions for a religious revolution. The logical standards are not, of course, the same as those of science and the ultimate test of truth is very different. Evidence for the emotions, not evidence for the senses, is the touchstone of religious truth. Deeply felt needs must be satisfied. Nevertheless, the parallels between scientific and religious conversion are much more impressive than the differences. Religious revolutions, too, may hold lessons for a theory of institutional revolution."[8]

While the parallels referred to here are real, they are not quite exact parallels. For one thing, religious belief rests on much more than an emotional foundation. For another, Catholic faith regards itself as the one true religious faith, as a result of which it has not only the right but the duty to take all possible steps within its power to make sure that it will continue undefiled. There is no room within it for religious revolution such as would compromise any of its basic tenets. It is for this reason that it always combats heresy.

For the same reason, it is bound to employ all possible and reasonable system support for the accomplishment of what it stands for. This can have relevance to Church-State relations. It certainly has relevance to Catholic education.

Nobody has written about this better than Peter Berger in his improbably-titled book, A *Rumor of Angels* (New York, 1969). As he puts it, only in a counter-community of considerable strength does cognitive deviance have a chance to flourish. In particular, theological surrender of the ends which it should serve to uphold, in the name of pluralism, progressiveness or whatever, defeats itself in precisely the measure of its success and ultimately ends in the self-liquidation of theology and of the institutions in which the theological tradition is embodied.

Those of us who have experienced the decline of Catholic publishing houses during the past ten years are only too well aware of the extent to which this has been caused by a self-generated support for the proliferation of books representing any and every kind of theological opinion, to the extent that the book-buying public — faced too with the cost of books nowadays — has decided that there is little point in buying such books at all.

As an aside in connection with this, may I say that I would like to see the old "Imprimatur" fully restored, so that Catholics can know what are Catholic books, that is, books that are free from doctrinal error, whether or not they may contain tentative opinions.

While exponents of the Catholic position have become latterly preoccupied with the need to update their presentations, they should not be blinded to the effects which their efforts can have in changing attitudes too radically. As Berger puts it: "Aggiornamento usually arises out of tactical considerations. It is argued that one must modify certain features of the institution or its message because otherwise one will not be able to reach this or that recalcitrant clientele—the intelligensia, or the working class, or the young. These modifications, however, entail a process of rethinking, the end results of which are hard to predict or control. Tactical modifications thus tend to escalate towards genuinely cognitive modifications. At this point the outside challenge becomes a challenge from within. The cognitive antagonist has crept inside the gates and, worse, inside the consciousness of the theologian assigned to guard the gates." [9]

It is, and rightly, Berger's contention that one of the fundamental prepositions of the sociology of knowledge is that the plausibility, in the sense of what people actually find credible, of views of whatsoever kind depends on the social support which these receive within the system which seeks to have them accepted. Every plausibility structure depends on its constituent elements—the people who pose as representing it, the "conversational" network by which they do so, the inherent ordering of the structure and so forth. [10]

He is quite outspoken to the effect that the maintenance of the Catholic faith in the consciousness of the individual believer requires that he maintain his relationship to the plausibility structure of Catholicism. But he is equally insistent that this entails as a correlative a community of Catholics in his social milieu who continually support his faith.

To quote him again: "Within this supportive community there will then be an ongoing conversation that, explicitly and implicitly, keeps a Catholic world going. Explicitly, there is affirmation, confirmation, reiteration of Catholic notions about reality. But there is also an implicit Catholicism in such a community. After all, in everyday life it is just as important that some things can silently be taken for granted as that some things are reaffirmed in so many words. Indeed, the most fundamental assumptions about the world are commonly affirmed by implication—they are so obvious that there is no need to put them into words. Our individual, then, operates within what may be called a specifically Catholic conversational apparatus, which, in innumerable ways, each day affirms the Catholic world that he cohabits with his significant others. If all these social mechanisms function properly, his Catholicism will be as natural to him as the color of his hair or his belief in the law of gravity. He will, indeed, be the happy possessor of an *anima naturaliter christiana*, a 'naturally Christian soul.'"[11]

To be sure, Berger is aware that this kind of flawlessness in the plausibility structure is not always easy to attain. It depends on the contribution of such elements as the authority within the system and the staff of educators who mediate to the individual, the details of which vary in different circumstances. But he is quite definite that the plausibility of Catholicism hinges upon the availability of these social determinants. The message for Catholic teachers— whether at higher or lower level—should be clear.

Education as Research

It has to be admitted that, in the domain of theological research, the problem is more complicated. By its very essence research implies more freedom than straightforward teaching. There are the requirements of a deeper plumbing of the subject matter, the search for new understanding compatible with the basic truths of faith, the effort at an "inculturation" of these truths into ways of thinking and conceptualizing that are different in different places among different peoples and at different times in human history.

The problem arises from the fact that the boundaries which are imposed by the Magisterium as the guardian — to use an old phrase — of the "deposit of faith" must be respected by the researcher as much as by the pedagogue.

Much has been and continues to be made in recent years by some theologians about the unacceptability of this restriction from the point of view of the academic freedom which should go hand in hand with theology as a science.

I would like to place on record the erroneous nature of such argumentation as seen by both the sociology of knowledge and the methodology of the sciences in general. It is vitiated at the very root by a forgetfulness of the fact that all science is tied to certain presuppositions.

In the case of the physical sciences the fact is that one major theory dominates and indeed controls research and teaching in any field until gradually its deficiencies become widely recognized by reason of its failing to satisfy an increasing set of expectations from it. As a result, it is discarded in favor of a new theory. It was because of their relevance that Comte included theories as well as facts and laws in his tripartite understanding of the constituent elements of science. Examples of theoretical frameworks which have reigned and later been replaced extend from Copernican and Newtonian physics to Einsteinian and post-Einsteinian models of the universe. Underlying all such change is the fact that there is a common language between the scientists, agreed criteria of reason and logic, a common approach, in short, a common ideology, in the purest sense of the word.

The human sciences are even more clearly linked with dependence on ideology. Analysts of economic science, for example, lay stress on the fact that, as far as it is concerned, there are no trans-historical truths. Economic action appropriate to one age would be inappropriate to another. There are no economic theories, therefore, which would be appropriate to more than one age. The labor theory of value, to take but one instance, arose in the age of capitalism and could not have arisen before it for the very reason that previous economic systems were not obviously dependent on hired labor, whereas this was the foundation stone of capitalist society.[12] This observation could as easily be matched by analogues relating to Marxist or Keyensian economic theories, related respectively to the increasing misery of the proletariat or the general interaction of unemployment, interest and money.

Political science provides a superb example of dependence on an ideological framework. As somebody has said about it, the facts relating to it are, typically, normative, as scarcely any factual statement can be made within the scope of politics in its usual sense without also involving values. As a further consequence, political theories, as it were, "secrete" values and there is no point pretending otherwise.[13]

Psychology also provides plenty of evidence to the effect that it too is ideologically predetermined. This has been expounded in a most articulate and personal way by Professor Hudson of Exeter College, Oxford, Cambridge University and later the Institute for Advanced Study at Princeton—a man who combines, at one and the same time, an expertise in the domains of both psychology and education.

Hudson writes: "Just as novelists draw on their experience, so too do psychologists. We would both be cut off, otherwise, from the springs of our intellectual vitality. To refuse a psychologist access to his intuitions, even if this were possible, would be as stultifying and as short-sighted as it would be to deny them to a physicist or a painter. Such immediate personal involvement becomes troublesome only when we try to conceal it...."[14]

Hudson is very interesting on the scientific approach to psychology which prevailed in his student days at Oxford (which, by the way, were more or less around the same time as I myself was a student there). The hidden ideology on which he was weaned, he says, was that imported into Britain from the United States after the Second World War, a mixture of the pragmatism of Dewey and the phenomenology of people like Freud who, although a European, was so espoused by American psychologists. Side by side with this, he was confronted with the Anglo-Saxon tradition in philosophy, at once enriched and confused by the contributions of Locke and Hume, Russell and Ayer, Ryle and many others — yet predominantly empirical and analytical, where the American and European slant was metaphysical and phenomenological. As a result of his learning experience, he quickly came to the conclusion that allegiances within psychology — what we have been referring to here as ideologies — are very real indeed.[15]

He was later to be reinforced in this persuasion when he came up against the Langian approach, this time more specifically European in color, more influenced by Sartre and the Existentialists than the analysts after the mode of Wittgenstein. He goes so far as to say that the conception of psychology pursued by Lang is so remote from that which was presented to him when a young student "that, comparing them, it is hard to believe that they can have even a verbal label — 'psychology' — in common."[16]

The presuppositions on which the supposedly more factual sciences of sociology and history are based are even more striking. There is no need for me to go into the once-agitated argument as to whether sociology is a value-free discipline: it is now accepted that it is not, never was, and cannot be such. The very positivism which acknowledged only value-excluded data was itself deeply value-orientated, if negatively.[17]

As regards history, I recall my own days at Oxford, when I took part in a weekly seminar in Merton College conducted by the able student of the philosophy of history, W.H. Walsh, which was centered — in the climate of that time — in analytical investigation, asking questions such as whether it is possible for people who are heir to a particular terminology and conceptualization to write any history which meaningfully describes the happenings of previous ages that are remotely removed from the historians intellectually. To me at least it was clear that the only conclusion was that if history is to be written at all it must rest on the presupposition that the terms and concepts which it employs are applicable.[18]

All of this is but a lengthy prelude to maintaining the thesis that theology too as a science is not only entitled to but must rest on its own presuppositions. Without more ado these can be said, in the case of Catholic theology, to be the assent of the theologian to the Catholic faith as asserted to him by the concurrent role of the authority of the Magisterium. At rock-bottom my argument is that Catholic theology as a science is unavoidably based on this substratum.

The correctness of this argument cannot be illustrated better than by way of reference to one of the indispensable sub-sciences of theology, namely, hermeneutics. One of the most important essays penned by the Dominican theologian, Fr. Edward Schillebeeckx, is that entitled "Towards a Catholic Use of Hermeneutics."[19] In this he points out most convincingly that, even though it is often thought that what is called the new hermeneutics, represented by non-Catholic scholars such as Bultmann and others, constitutes an unbridgeable gap with its predecessors, in that it seeks to interpret Scripture in terms of the condition of contemporary man, the fact is that it has always been a keystone of Catholic theology to strive to express the message of God to men in a specific historical situation.

What is not sufficiently realized is that the Catholic contribution to the development of dogma, as for example, the Christological dogma of Chalcedon, implies that the scriptural evidence is something to be interpreted in the light of the Church's experience, as it then was against the backdrop of the fifth century, but in a way that consistently expresses the same datum of faith that is given to us in the Scriptures. The same thing can be said in different ways, but only to the extent that the theologian gives allegiance to that primordial datum.

To bring the matter down to its bare requirements, the fact is that the Catholic theologian's understanding of the text of the Bible, insofar as he employs hermeneutics to that end, must be something which has grown out of the past, though directed to the present. His self-understanding in that present has to be intimately embedded in his received understanding of the faith.

It is well to be aware of what this implies for his use of hermeneutics. It does not mean that when Trent laid down that "it is the Church's prerogative to judge the true sense and interpretation of the Sacred Scriptures," it meant to declare that the Church's apostolic office is the hermeneutical principle. Rather is the position that this office is the judge of our Catholic hermeneutical application in the interpretation of the faith by working on the Bible. What I am trying to say — following Schillebeeckx's remarkable insight into all this — is that whereas, undoubtedly, Catholic theological employers of hermeneutics have to be concerned with the hermeneutical significance of their own distance in time from the composition of the Scriptures, this distance is in no way a void but is filled by the continuity of tradition. This means that the submission of the interpreter to the scriptural text takes place not only within the context of ideas and terms characteristic of his existential reality but also by a present that has been formed by a larger past.

Schillebeeckx says that the science of hermeneutics, as an open system of critique, is made possible not by ignoring our own background but rather by the direct opposite—admitting that the light which the scholar may throw on any text in his turn cannot preempt the antecedent judgments of which he is also an inheritor because he is situated in history and lives from the past to the present and into the future. These presuppositions are not eliminated but on the contrary reinforced by this, by reason of which he must approach texts from a preunderstanding of what he is doing and must continually remain conscious of the fact that this approach means confronting the text with his own preunderstanding. "The insight that man is, because of his historicity, in a tradition, and that his freedom is limited, among other things, by the factuality of this past is therefore fundamental to hermeneutics."[20] Thereby is provided the frame of reference within which questions should be asked and answered. In it we have a consciousness of time that also transcends temporality.

But I need not labor the matter. It ends up with a persuasion that Catholic theology, even in respect of its infra-structure of procedural apparatus, is a conditioned thing while yet remaining, like all other sciences, a true science.

Like them it is suffused with ideology, an ideology which, after the manner of all ideology, is both "dogmatic" and "action-oriented." For it is the function of ideologies, beliefs if you wish, to protect the minds of their adherents from what they regard as falsehood and equally to seek that they act in a way that does not contradict these beliefs. It is because of his awareness of this that Shils, in his article in the *International Encyclopedia of the*

Social Sciences, claims that ideology is always concerned with authority and is always, therefore, in some sense "political" ideology. This holds for both its manifest and latent functions.

Once again the message for Catholic educators — this time specifically for Catholic educators as researchers — should be clear.

Let us look, therefore, in conclusion, to the role of the Magisterium as authority in the Church in relation to Catholic ideology or faith as the presupposition of Catholic higher education, indeed of Catholic education of all kinds.

The Role of Authority

Concerning this we can with profit hark back to David Bell's book, mentioned earlier, for some ideas about power, influence and authority.

Take firstly power and influence. Power is best described as a communication to do something on the basis of a hypothetical threat or promise. Its request might be expressed in the form, to take the example: "If you construct a building badly, I will deprive you of your builder's license." Influence is more a sanction-free communication to do something and might be expressed, following our example, in the form: "If you construct a building badly, you are in danger of a serious accident."

The difference between power and influence is that power presupposes control over some resource that can serve as a sanction, while influence rests on bases which help the influencer to change others, influences such as the prestige of the influencer (in virtue of his position) or the prestige of his message (in virtue of its inherent rationality).

At times, power and influence can be difficult to disentangle, yet the distinction between them is there.

At times too either of them can have a tacit effect in that the receiver of the communication can have an "anticipatory reaction" about the likely outcome of his action. In fact, by and large, to the extent that he is socialized, he will tend to anticipate reactions to his actions. As Bell puts it: "To the extent that we have learned to be 'sociable' animals, we continually anticipate others' reactions to our own behavior. In a sense, sociability implies precisely this consciousness of the social context in which we live.... Through anticipation, we internalize a sense of society which tacitly and invisibly controls our behavior."[21]

Authority differs from both "power" and "influence" in that instead of being hypothetical or contingent in its communication, it is of its very nature categorical or imperative, taking the form of "Do this" or "Don't do that." Thus, to follow our earlier example, it would say quite clearly: "Construct buildings properly," or, "Do not construct buildings carelessly."

But it should be noted carefully that authority can be transformed into either power or influence by expressing itself by way of a hypothetical equivalent rather than by a categorical command based on a moral imperative. Indeed all too often secular authority, especially in the State, reduces itself to power in this way, a distortion of authority in the true sense.

It is undeniable that authority is usually associated with the possession of sanction application — what Bell calls its "miranda" — as, for example, when a government is backed by a show of physical force. But more appropriate to it, as the right to moral persuasion, is what Bell calls its "credenda," namely, the assent that it can expect in its support, such as the conviction of people that it represents a sound framework for their ordered behavior.

It is a feature of our time that the credenda of authority in general have (and rightly) come to be appreciated more than its "miranda." This is very evident in the secular world, where rulers are progressively being compelled for one reason or another to give evidence of sound reasons for their directives. The developments are such that acceptance of authority on this assumption is rapidly coming to be seen as part of socialization in civilized society. Related to it is the consequence that traditional attitudes of authority concerning the positions and values of the past can also be accepted by people as long as they permit of a similar internalization and conscious personal articulation as against a nonparticipatory submission.

For what it is worth, I believe that this change in the secular world in respect of authority should have repercussions on the use of authority in the Church. Specifically, what I am saying is that, whereas in the past all too frequently the authority of the Magisterium was reduced to the exercise of power, as in the case of Savonarola, Galileo and many others in earlier times and that of some Modernist thinkers in the first quarter of this century, in the present climate of opinion it would do much better, while retaining its canon of imperativity, to seek to reduce itself in practice more to influence rather than power.

This in truth seems to be what is taking place at the moment in cases such as those of Professor Kung and Archbishop Lefebvre. Be this as it may, I trust that I have adduced sufficient reasons from the human sciences—leaving theology aside—to make it evident that Catholic higher education should maintain a close and essential relationship with the Magisterium, the teaching authority of the Church.

Footnotes

1. R. Coffy, "Magisterium and Theology," *The Irish Theological Quarterly* XLIII (1976) 255-6.

2. *Loc. cit.*, 10-11.

3. In *Harvard Educational Review* 40 (1970), n. 2.

4. Cf. A. Morrison and D. McIntyre, *Schools and Socialization*, London, 1971, Ch. 3.

5. Cf. R. and A.E.M. Seaborne, *The Psychology of Learning*, London, 1966, Ch. 11.

6. Boyer and Seaborne, *op. cit.*, 211.

7. See M. Brewster Smith, *"Attitude Change,"* in N. Warren, M. Jahoda, edd., *Attitudes* (London, 1973).

8. E. Reimer, *School Is Dead* (London, 1971) 140-141.

9. Berger, *op. cit.*, 36-37.

10. *Op. cit.*, 50ff.

11. *Op. cit.*, 52-53.

12. Cf. H.M. Drucker, *The Political Uses of Ideology* (London, 1974) 24.

13. Drucker, *op. cit.*, 37.

14. L. Hudson, *The Cult of the Fact*, London, 1972, p. 129.

15. *Op. cit.*, pp. 80-81.

16. *Op cit.*, p. 76.

17. Cf. J. Newman, *Introduction to Sociology* (Dublin, 1972) 17-24.

18. W.H. Walsh, *An Introduction to the Philosophy of History* (London, 1951).

19. E. Schillebeeckx, "Towards a Catholic Use of Hermeneutics," in *God and the Future of Man* (London, 1969).

20. *Op. cit.*, p. 27.

21. Bell, *op. cit.*, p. 34.

CHAPTER SEVEN

The Magisterium
and Catholic Higher Education

Abbot Edmund McCaffrey, OSB

Colleges and insane asylums are both mental institutions in a way—but one has to show some improvement to graduate from an asylum! Well, I am not too sure of the present condition of our mental institutions, but the condition of Catholic higher education is patently evident: there is a common link, Catholic higher education has gone crazy!

To be crazy is to be disordered; to be unsound; it means to be extremely foolish. Well, when Catholic institutions and educators separate themselves from the Magisterium, we can rightly say they are disordered, unsound and foolish for they have departed from their purpose and their very reason of being. They have departed from a divinely established source of truth.

How distressed the laity have been in the last ten years or so! How often have we heard them reflect: "If there is no Catholic milieu on campus and if Catholic principles are not taught, why should they go to college X?" They realize they can get the same education elsewhere much cheaper and with less danger to the Faith of the student.

Basically what faces us today in Catholic higher education is precisely the problem that has recently plagued a major automobile manufacturer. It seems incredible, but automobiles of one brand name were sold but contained engines of another model. It does not take much ethical acumen to determine that this is theft pure and simple—a great rip-off! Sound business practice demands and requires *truth in advertising.* Truth in advertising is very important.

How much more important is truth necessary when we are dealing with the immaterial—with the minds and souls of persons. Yet in the educational arena we are experiencing a similar rip-off like the one in the automobile industry; only the consequences and implications are greater. Some Catholic institutions of higher education that identify themselves as "Catholic" are giving a different product than that which is advertised. I call this both an intellectual and moral rip-off!

The pattern in these institutions is all too familar: Catholic theology classes bear little semblance to magisterial teaching, and when the Church's teachings are presented they are made to seem as "options" that may be selected but second best at most to the speculations of theologians X and Y; school newspapers which are supported by the institution or controlled by it (lack of control might be a better description) present abortion ads, use vulgar four-letter words, ridicule Church teachings and in general display an outstanding degree of bad taste. Speakers are selected because of avant-garde views or because their views are opposed to the Church's; dormitory and campus living standards lack civility, good taste and moral guidance; and "living together"—if not outright accepted—is at least implicitly condoned. Academic freedom for these institutions means permissiveness. Any pronouncement of absolutes and moral norms sends tremors of terror down the spines of administrators—if, indeed, they have any spines at all. And so on and on we can go, the litany is all too familiar.

The environment and philosophy of such institutions is relative and behavioral. For those who understand the roots of behavioralism recognize that this means a gross materialism. Roots seem to be a big thing today—to find our roots; well, let me say that part of our problem is *philosophical* and we have abandoned our philosophical roots which identify absolutes. But you see, we have watered-down our philosophical curriculum so that the subtleties of behavioralism are missed by many until this philosophy has become so entrenched—so much a part of the person and the environment—that it becomes exceedingly difficult to oppose it effectively or to overcome it.

The last twelve years or so have been disastrous for Catholic higher education in the United States, for Catholic teaching and values have been distilled from the teaching and environment by the behavioral thrust. What we have produced are religious and moral illiterates. It seems that every philosophical and theological school of thought and their proponents have a luminous charism, but the very Institution founded by Jesus Himself and His appointed Vicar on earth lack any sort of charism! Theologian X, because his views are popular and have a numerically great following, is rated higher than the Pope—the man Christ promised to guide with His Holy Spirit. This state of affairs is incredible! Is this not arrogance? Pride and arrogance are a natural corollary of behavioralism, for behavioralism places greater reliance on quantitative data than on the qualitative—on the material rather than the immaterial or spiritual. The support of numbers seems to puff up.

Authenticity is the name of the game. Catholic higher education must be from first to last authentic. The word "authentic" scares some for they fear some kind of outdated, stuffy "conservatism." This is not the meaning. To be authentic is to be committed to the truth—to embrace the entire Gospel message. It means respecting magisterial ministry. This means embracing the See of Peter, for the successors of

Peter are the Vicars of Jesus, and Catholic higher education must teach as Jesus taught. This is the will of Jesus. It means listening to Paul VI because when I see Paul, I see Jesus. This is not childish servility; it is His will.

To be authentic then means not to subvert or change the official teaching of the Holy Father and the Church. It means embracing, at times, the unpopular: i.e., to be *against* abortion—to be *for* Humanae Vitae.

In short, to be authentic means at times to be in the minority; it means judging by God's standards, not by man's. Remember that passage in St. Mark's Gospel? Jesus talks of judging by man's standards rather than God's. The apostles and Jews looked for a Messiah who would be king, who would come in power and majesty. This, however, was not God's way. Listen: "Jesus began to teach them that the Son of Man had to suffer much, be rejected by the elders, the chief priests, and the scribes, be put to death and rise three days later. He said these things quite openly. Peter took him aside and began to remonstrate with him. At this he turned around and, eying the disciples, reprimanded Peter: 'Get out of my sight, you satan! You are not judging by God's standards but by man's' "² (Mk. 8:27ff.).

A main problem facing Catholic higher education today is found precisely here: we are using man's standard's rather than God's. Part of the responsibility for the mess Catholic higher education finds itself in can be laid at the feet of Catholic leaders. In my own association with bishops, superiors and others I have frequently heard great murmurings of concern about the qualitative changes that have taken place in Catholic institutions of higher learning. Often the utterances have not been of mere concern but were of outrage at the blatant dilution of Catholic values.

I must candidly say that some of the problems or their intensity can be placed at the feet of the bishops themselves. It is my opinion that in some instances a few bishops have failed to exercise strong and dynamic leadership in Catholic higher education, or while they expressed concern they failed to exercise their legitimate prerogatives in this vital area. Grave concerns about other important questions sidetracked their attention and they seemed as a result to be indifferent to the plight of these institutions. Some just failed to watch the store! This is not a pastoral way of acting or thinking.

The Directory on the Pastoral Ministry of Bishops clearly indicates the need for episcopal awareness and concern:

"If he has any higher institution of ecclesiastical studies or a Catholic University in his diocese, the bishop cherishes it with special affection and carefully fulfills his. office and duties in its regard, especially as far as his magisterium is concerned.... He encourages pastoral activity in every university, also the non-Catholic university, and wisely makes this pastoral action a part of the organized program of the whole diocese, observing the norms given by the episcopal conference and by the Apostolic See. In all things he strives that faith and good morals are correctly taught, promoted and safeguarded."[1]

One bishop told me the way he handled a Catholic institution of higher learning was just to ignore it. Well, at times, ignoring a situation may be the best strategy, but certainly not when the magisterium is totally ignored and where contrary teachings prevail. This is poor leadership! Does not the Directory clearly state that the bishop must strive to see that "faith and good morals are correctly taught, promoted and safeguarded"?

Ignoring a situation is often bad teaching, for it misleads many into believing that error is condoned.

It is interesting to note that in the same *Directory* some general principles of pastoral rule are laid down. These fundamental principles include one that is almost forgotten today in all forms of governing, vis., the *Principle of the Common Good.* This principle, of course, is at odds with behavioral philosophy, for in behavioral thought either the individual good takes precedence or a behavioral common good is concocted and determined by numerical superiority or popular applause. (Hence, the rejection of *Humanae Vitae* and papal teaching on sexual morality.)

It must always be remembered that the common good of the diocese "is ordained to the good of the universal Church and takes precedence over that of more particular communities of the diocese."[2] At the same time, in dealing with these often very delicate matters arising in the complex academic world, one must avoid hindering a particular legitimate good. Bishops and superiors need always remember these three other important principles, vis.:

1. *The Principle of Responsible Cooperation,* where the bishop in ruling readily recognizes and preserves the just liberty both of individuals and groups and willingly shares with others the sense of both individual and group responsibility in carrying out their duties.[3]

2. *The Principle of Subsidiarity.* Here the bishop does not ordinarily take to himself what can well be performed by others. The *Directory* puts it well: "He carefully respects the legitimate competencies of others and also gives his co-workers the powers they need and favors the just initiatives of individual believers and of groups."[4]

3. *The Principle of Coordination.* The *Directory* explains that "the bishop considers it his duty not only to stir up, encourage and increase the energies within his diocese, but also to weld them together so as to avoid harmful scattering and useless duplica-

tions as well as destructive dissensions, while at
the same time always preserving the lawful rights
and liberty of the faithful."[5]

Let me digress for a moment on this fundamental
principle of pastoral rule. What I have to say is
delicate and controversial and in no way is it meant
to be judgmental. In the arena of Catholic higher
education in the United States there is a profound
dissatisfaction among the faithful with many existing
institutions because they have abandoned their
roots and Catholic identity. This sometimes gives
rise to reactions which in themselves are not pro-
ductive or beneficial to a suitable remedy. Faced
with a seemingly hopeless task of reformation of
existing structures, the impulse is to "let us begin
anew." Indeed this may be necessary and desirable,
but generally I believe this should not be the direction.

While one can understand the rationale, sym-
pathize with new pioneers and recognize their
right to blaze new frontiers, nevertheless, it is my
personal opinion that this should not be the ordinary
method of approach today. I would hate to see this
become a trend. Why?

1. All institutions have not abandoned their
Catholic identity. Likewise there are some which
while leaning in a dangerous direction can be salvaged if an effort is made. We have a duty to help
them.

2. We live in an era of scarcity of personnel and
resources, hence, in the words of the *Directory*,
we must "avoid harmful scattering and useless
duplication."

3. The promotion of unity is not always served.
"Destructive dissension" should be avoided if
at all possible without, however, sacrificing the
liberty of others and the common good.

4. Beginning anew involves a tremendous
effort—an effort that might well be spent on helping

those who are trying to keep their identity and those capable of being salvaged. Great resources are needed today to begin a new institution of higher education. The problems that must be faced are: material problems, faculty problems, recruitment problems, accreditation problems, etc., and it is my humble opinion that these efforts and resources ought to be spent on those institutions on the brink of closing that desire to follow the magisterium and keep their Catholic identity.

There can be listed other reasons, but I believe these are sufficient to show the direction we should take in these days of uncertainty.

Another very interesting principle of pastoral rule is enunciated in the *Directory*, which I believe is very important with respect to the magisterium and Catholic higher education. It is called the *Principle of Placing the Right People in the Right Places*. What is meant by this? The *Directory* explains:

"In making use of the human resources of those who cooperate in ruling the Church, the bishop is led by supernatural considerations, and pursuing above all the good of souls he preserves the dignity of persons by employing their talents in as fitting and useful a way as possible for the service of the community and by placing the right person in the right place."[6]

The right person in the right place—this takes diplomacy and courage! Catholic higher education can definitely be enhanced and the magisterium positively promoted by religious superiors, administrators and bishops implementing this rule. If Father X has a promise or vow of obedience and if he is found teaching contrary to the Magisterium, then it is time for a change! Bishops and superiors have not hesitated to transfer priests at given intervals and at times quickly if the actions of individuals are detrimental to the parish, group or financial health. Why don't they do the same for the University? Delicate? Yes; problems with tenure? Yes; but it is better to have six months or a year of ruckus than a decade of insidious destruction. Where are the Ordinaries and religious superiors of men and women who are allowed to remain in university and seminary positions and thereby add prestige to theological speculations at odds with the Magisterium? For religious, exemption does not mean autonomy; it does not exempt one from the legitimate authority of the bishop (the center and source of unity in the diocese) or from Magisterium teaching. Academic freedom is not a higher value than God's truth or the teaching proclaimed by His Church.

This principle of placing the right people in the right places is extremely important and has deep pastoral implications. The exercise of this principle can save many souls. To some Ordinaries and religious superiors I say, try it!

Another area of consideration for preventing the loss of Catholic identity in Catholic higher education and for preserving unity relates to *structural* questions. One of the greatest heresies today is the implicit denial of original sin by dreamers who somehow have drifted from the real world. There are many good people who in some utopian dream believe that *presence alone* will be sufficient to preserve Catholic identity and the integrity of the Magisterium. Presence alone, however, is not sufficient as experience has shown — structure also is necessary.

Since Vatican II the theories of ownership of ecclesiastical institutions put forth by the late Msgr. John McGrath have received wide acceptance and have, I believe, been disastrous for the religious bodies themselves and for the Church at large. McGrath stated: "If anyone owns the assets of the charitable or educational institution, it is the general public. Failure to appreciate this fact has led to the mistaken idea that the property of the institution is the property of the sponsoring body."[7] Here we have a beautiful formula for secularization!

This premise has resulted in religious bodies being alienated from their apostolates; it has caused a loss of interest in individual community members in their apostolic work; it has encouraged the loss of religious control in their apostolates and has resulted in a disenfranchisement (often contrary to Canon Law) of religious communities.

Father Adam Maida paints the results of structural changes flowing from the McGrath Thesis vividly in these terms:

"And so it was that many institutions changed their charters and bylaws, changed the character of their institutions, transferred control of their institutions to lay boards, and thus successfully disenfranchised their religious congregations and Church. The various religious congregations which gave birth to these institutions, nurtured them, funded them, staffed them, controlled them, and made them effective witnesses of the love of God for man through religion, now find a witness which has been dissipated, an apostolate which has been lost, an ownership which has been alienated and an experience which has become a nightmare."[8]

A positive step in support of the Magisterium and to insure its acceptance will be achieved if we carefully structure our institutions to insure their rightful identity and ownership. Likewise those religious communities that have given up control should seek to regain it wherever possible so that fidelity to the Christian message as it comes to us through the Church will be insured.

I believe a very positive approach to the problem arising from the relationship of the Magisterium to

Catholic higher education can be summed up in Edmund Burke's saying about statesmen, vis., "My idea of a statesman is one who can accept what is good of the past and build upon it." Just change the word "statesman" to "Catholic educator."

Accepting what is good of the past means those absolutes, those eternal truths, the Church and her teachings. Building upon the past is the continuing contributions of the various sciences and legitimate theological speculation.

I believe John Henry Newman reflects this approach in a most beautiful way.[9] He can well be taken today as a model and inspiration for Catholic educators in this changing world. In the last decade or so we have experienced a decay that is extensive and pervasive—the crisis is severe, yet it is not fatal. The educational consciousness presented by Newman is not "new" but it does entail the restoration of "old" educational first principles. Newman enunciates the basic and essential elements of an intellectual consciousness which aims at excellence in higher education. This consciousness is made up of civility, opened and reasoned discourse, disciplined scholarship, inspired teaching, and that abiding quest for permanent things. *Concerning civility* of an educated person Newman wrote: "He knows when to speak and when to be silent; he is able to converse, he is able to listen; he can ask a question pertinently, and gain a lesson seasonably." And again: "It is well to be a gentleman, it is well to have a cultivated intellect, a delicate taste, a candid, equitable, dispassionate mind, a noble and courteous bearing in the conduct of life—these are the connatural qualities of a large knowledge; they are the objects of a university."

Yet civility is not enough—one is quite capable of degenerating into an elegant imbecile. So to civility Newman adds the concept of *Opened and reasoned discourse.* He notes that a university "is a place of concourse.... It is a place where inquiry is pushed forward, and discoveries verified and perfected, and rashness rendered innocuous, and error exposed, by the collision of mind with mind, and knowledge with knowledge."

To civility and discourse Newman adds *discipline* — something that Americans in particular seem to flee from. Learning is not without exertion and toil, for he notes: "Discipline is imperative, if the mind is to discriminate substance from shadows." He notes that "the bodily eye, the organ for apprehending material objects, is provided by nature; the eye of the mind, of which the object is truth, is the work of discipline and habit."

Next he adds *excellence in teaching*. "An academical system without the personal influence of teachers upon pupils is an arctic winter; it will create an ice-bound, petrified, cast-iron university, and nothing else."

Finally Newman indicates the importance and indispensability of *"the permanent things."* For him, knowledge alone is not sufficient but religious content was needed to give direction, meaning and completeness to the accumulation of knowledge. He argues for a Biblical View, and to those who fear that the intellect would be crushed by dogma he says: "Some persons will say that I am thinking of confining, distorting, and stunting the growth of the intellectual by ecclesiastical supervision. I have no such thought.... I wish the intellect to range with the utmost freedom, and religion to enjoy an equal freedom; but what I am stipulating for is that they should be found in one and the same place, and exemplified in the same persons. I want to destroy that diversity of centers which puts everything into confusion by creating a contrariety of influences... I want the intellectual layman to be religious, and the devout ecclesiastic to be intellectual."

Doesn't Newman bring the Magisterium and the education enterprise into wonderful harmony? The problems are basically *spiritual* and *philosophical*. The Magisterium rightly understood gives integrity to the academy.

John Kennedy once said: "A child miseducated is a child lost." Some might say we have lost a generation in our seminaries, colleges and schools but the future is not lost if we do this:

1. Communicate the authentic message of Christ. That we strive to be what the Church wants us to be — truly Catholic.

2. That we be open to the world and to modern problems, fostering dialogue with all forms of culture — with atheists, non-Christians, and with Christians of various confessions.

3. That while being open to the modern world, we maintain fully the "Catholic" character of our institutions.

4. And that consequently, in the classroom, in publications, in all areas of academic life we provide for complete orthodoxy of teaching and for obedience to the magisterium of the Church and for fidelity to the hierarchy and the Holy See.

These provisions should be incorporated into the statutes of our institutions in such a way as to be valid before the civil law.

If we do this we give testimony to the Faith we profess. It does not mean you are unaware of the problems in administering truly Catholic institutions, but rather it gives you strength of conviction to meet these problems in a balanced way. If we follow Christ and His Church we cannot go wrong.

Footnotes

1. *Directory on the Pastoral Ministry of Bishops,* Publications Service of the Canadian Catholic Conference, Ottawa, Ontario, 1974, par. 68.

2. *Ibid.*, par. 93.
3. *Ibid.*, par. 95.
4. *Ibid.*, par. 96.
5. *Ibid.*, par. 97.
6. *Ibid.*, par. 98.
7. John J. McGrath, *Catholic Institutions in the United States: Canonical and Civil Law Status,* Catholic University of America Press, Washington, D.C., 1968, p. 33.
8. Rev. Adam J. Maida, "Canon Law/Civil Law Status of Catholic Hospitals," Address at Catholic Health Assembly, Denver, June 1973 (Reprinted in *Hospital Progress,* August 1973). See also, Rev. Adam Maida, "Ownership, Control, and Sponsorship of Catholic Institutions," Pennsylvania Catholic Conference, Harrisburg, Pa., 1975.
9. John Henry Newman, "Idea of a University, Defined and Illustrated," London, 1853.

Also available from St. Paul Editions

The Sacrament of Penance in Our Time
Edited by George A. Kelly

In-depth lectures on the sacrament of Reconciliation covering such topics as: Socio-historical questions about the penitential discipline of the Catholic Church; Penance and the Second Vatican Council; The New Rite of Penance; Penance as renewal and reconciliation, etc. Contributors to this timely book are Robert I. Bradley, S.J., Bruce A. Williams, O.P., Joseph E. Hogan, C.M., Eugene Kevane, John A. Hardon, S.J.
165 pages; cloth $4.00; paper $3.00

The Catechism of Modern Man
Edited and compiled by a team of Daughters of St. Paul
Best Seller
—Over 9,000 topics—**The Catechism of Modern Man** is the only complete source of the Council's new and profound expression of the Faith—all in the words of Vatican II and related post-conciliar documents.
731 pages; plastic or cloth $6.95; paper $5.95

The 16 Documents of Vatican II
The paperback and plastic edition includes a topical index and commentaries from outstanding Council Fathers.
760 pages; cloth or plastic $3.75; paper $3.00

The Dynamic Voice of Vatican II
(A paraphrase of the 16 Documents of Vatican II)

Edited by Marina Ruffolo

In the hope of bringing Vatican Council II's dynamic voice to all men, its sixteen documents have been paraphrased in an easy-to-read version, not as a substitute, but as an encouragement to read the documents themselves.
304 pages; cloth $4.50; paper $2.95

The Church's Amazing Story
Daughters of St. Paul

Concise and up-to-date, this volume offers an objective, balanced view of the Church in every age, highlighting outstanding events and personalities in a vivid, honest manner. Another feature—continuity without extraneous dates and material. And because many profit greatly by viewing the happenings of today in the light of history, notes are provided at chapter endings to personalize and spiritualize the lessons of yesterday for the reader on the current scene.
269 pages; cloth $4.00; paper $3.00

The Catholic Church Through the Ages
Rev. Martin P. Harney, S.J.

Thorough and factual. The author, historian and long-time Church history professor, treats every major issue from the era of primitive Christianity up into our own twentieth century. His style reveals his familiarity with the events he relates. Ideal as reference material, this newest work could also lend itself very well to classroom use.
600 pages; cloth $8.95; paper $7.95

Design for a Just Society

A brief, clear treatment of Catholic social teaching, including:

—the reasons why the Church speaks out on social issues;

—the dignity and rights of man;

—human solidarity and brotherhood;

—the vital importance of the family;

—the true role of the political community;

—the means of attaining and maintaining healthy and progressive economic life;

—guidelines for world development and peace.

Quotations from papal documents, Vatican II and Sacred Scripture give this volume a richness that may be increased still more by following up the abundant suggestions given for further reading. The discussion questions and project suggestions can lead to fruitful life applications.   cloth $4.00; paper $3.00

Visible Community of Love

Presents the Church in both her charismatic and structured aspects. Outstanding for their factual and balanced presentation are the sections on ecumenism and on the major non-Christian religions. Tenth graders will develop a healthy respect for other beliefs while gaining a deeper insight into various aspects of Catholic belief. Study questions included.

                          cloth $4.00; paper $3.00

The Church—Light of All Mankind
Pope Paul VI

Ecumenism; the nature, marks, and missionary vocation of the Church; the mission of the laity, the proper balance between concern for the world and the necessary detachment of the Christian whose goal is beyond this world; devotion to the Holy Spirit and

its relationship to respect for the visible Church; the importance of austerity, mortification and obedience to the vitality of the Church; these and other matters of similar relevance are treated.
156 pages; cloth $2.00

The Church in Our Day
The Bishops of the United States
A collective pastoral letter on the life and development of the American Catholic Church in the light of Vatican II. "A truly magnificent document. I earnestly trust that all our clergy, religious and laity will read and study it with great care." Most Rev. Bernard J. Flanagan, Bishop of Worcester, Ma.
104 pages; paperback 60c

Order from addresses on the following page.

Daughters of St. Paul

IN MASSACHUSETTS
    50 St. Paul's Avenue, Boston, Ma. 02130
    172 Tremont Street, Boston, Ma. 02111
IN NEW YORK
    78 Fort Place, Staten Island, N.Y. 10301
    59 East 43rd St., New York, N.Y. 10017
    625 East 187th Street, Bronx, N.Y. 10458
    525 Main Street, Buffalo, N.Y. 14203
IN NEW JERSEY
    Hudson Mall — Route 440 and
        Communipaw Ave., Jersey City, N.J. 07304
IN CONNECTICUT
    202 Fairfield Avenue, Bridgeport, Ct. 06604
IN OHIO
    2105 Ontario St. (at Prospect Ave.), Cleveland, Oh. 44115
    25 E. Eighth Street, Cincinnati, Oh. 45202
IN PENNSYLVANIA
    1719 Chestnut St., Philadelphia, Pa. 19103
IN FLORIDA
    2700 Biscayne Blvd., Miami, Fl. 33137
IN LOUISIANA
    4403 Veterans Memorial Blvd., Metairie, La. 70002
    1800 South Acadian Thruway, P.O. Box 2028,
        Baton Rouge, La. 70802
IN MISSOURI
    1001 Pine St. (at North 10th), St. Louis, Mo. 63101
IN TEXAS
    114 East Main Plaza, San Antonio, Tx. 78205
IN CALIFORNIA
    1570 Fifth Avenue, San Diego, Ca. 92101
    46 Geary Street, San Francisco, Ca. 94108
IN HAWAII
    1143 Bishop St., Honolulu, Hi. 96813
IN ALASKA
    750 West 5th Avenue, Anchorage, Ak. 99501
IN CANADA
    3022 Dufferin Street, Toronto 395, Ontario, Canada
IN ENGLAND
    57, Kensington Church Street, London W. 8, England
IN AUSTRALIA
    58, Abbotsford Rd., Homebush, N.S.W., Sydney 2140,
        Australia